THE ROGUES GALLERY

The aim of The Rogues Gallery is to bring history down to a private human-plane, to exhibit the colour and conduct of a given period through typical men and women. We shall present these Rogues, Scallywags, Eccentrics, Worthies and Villains in individual dossiers as examples of history, as people who contributed to the richness and colour of their time and who, before they ended at Execution Dock, Tyburn Tree, Newgate or peaceably in their beds, demonstrated clearly and often forcibly the state of Law, the venality of Politicians and Office-holders, the recklessness of Speculators, the public temper of their day.

DR. QUICKSILVER is the third in this series, the first was EDWARD WORTLEY MONTAGU, by Jonathan Curling and the second was CAPTAIN THOMAS JOHNSTONE by James Cleugh. Other titles in this series will be announced when they are ready.

DR. QUICKSILVER

1660-1742

BOOKS BY L. A. G. STRONG

Novels

    The Garden
    Sea Wall
    The Bay
    Trevannian
    The Brothers
    Hill of Howth
    etc.

Non-fiction

    The Minstrel Boy
    The Sacred River
    The Story of Sugar
    John McCormack; the Story of a Singer
    Commonsense about Drama
    etc.

Poems

    Lowery Road
    Northern Lights
    etc.

THOMAS DOVER, M.D., RESCUING ALEXANDER
SELKIRK (*ROBINSON CRUSOE*)

THE ROGUES GALLERY NUMBER THREE

DR. QUICKSILVER

1660–1742

The Life and Times of Thomas Dover, M.D.

L. A. G. STRONG

With 18 illustrations reproduced in collotype

ANDREW MELROSE
Stratford Place London

Andrew Melrose Limited

London   Melbourne   Sydney   Auckland
Bombay   Cape Town   New York   Toronto

First published 1955

Collotype by L. Van Leer & Co. Ltd.
Set in eleven point Monotype Baskerville
one point leaded
Printed in Great Britain
by The Anchor Press, Ltd.,
Tiptree, Essex

LIST OF ILLUSTRATIONS

FOREWORD

No life of Thomas Dover has previously been attempted, although there have been various short accounts and sketches of him, particulars of which will be found in the bibliography. In several instances a lack of positive information has made it difficult to check the points in which these documents differ: but the discrepancies are nowhere serious.

I have been frankly inconsistent in the matter of spelling. Dover himself, and the chroniclers Cooke and Woodes Rogers, on whom we have to rely for our knowledge of the famous voyage, did not trouble much about consistency, so that we need not regard their versions of familiar words as sacred. Often contemporary spelling gives to past histories a spurious air of quaintness which can be damaging when the narrative deals with practical matters. I have accordingly modernized Woodes Rogers' spelling, and some of Cooke's, leaving intact passages where the literary value seemed to depend, in part at any rate, on the original spelling.

I owe a great debt to a number of people who have helped me. Miss Jessica Jenkins, M.A. (Oxon) has been responsible for most of the research, and my secretary Mrs. Herbert Ochs, M.A. (Oxon), for the rest, and for other assistance without which I could not get on at all. I give my grateful thanks to them and to Mr. W. S. Haugh, B.A., F.L.A., Librarian of Bristol; the Harveian Librarian of the Royal College of Physicians; the Librarian of the Royal College of Surgeons; Dr. D. N. Phear, for permission to quote from an article; Mr. Patrick Pringle, for valuable suggestions and advice; and, finally, my good friend Mr. James Whittaker, who not only suggested a subject but gave a number of most valuable references for research and reading.

For the illustrations I acknowledge gratefully the permission given by the British Museum, the Royal College of Physicians, the Royal College of Surgeons and *Picture Post* Library to reproduce material in their possession.

L. A. G. S.

ONE

D ELIBERATELY chosen, the title and subtitle of this book are exact in their statement of its aim, if not of its achievement. The title is a nickname, the label tied to Dr. Dover by his contemporaries. It was based on one propensity in a character so hard to come at, that, until more material is discovered, any biography of him must be a bare account of what we know him to have done, and a sketch of the times in which he did it. The sketch is essential, if we are to get any reasonable view of him: hence the subtitle.

A successful medical practitioner, born, according to the best supported of three statements, in 1662, Dover turned aside from his work, became for three years a privateer, shared in the rescue of Alexander Selkirk, returned to medicine with a large fortune in prize money and the bias which earned him his nickname, to spend his last active years in violent and sometimes scurrilous medical controversy. Such a man seems to us more like a figure from a comic opera than a pioneer in objective clinical work and the inventor of a prescription which, after two hundred years, is still in the pharmacopoeia. Viewed against twentieth-century standards the career of Thomas Dover does not make sense. In his own day he was no more an anomaly than certain individualists who are looked at askance or wryly admired in London clubs today. He was a character, *un originel*, but he fitted into his background and was proper to his time.

Any attempt to make sense of such a character comes up first of all against the central problem which confronts all biographers when they try to give life to a figure from a bygone age. A man and his background are a whole. Everything he thinks and says and does is rooted in the world of which he is a part. What he is, the fabric of his individuality, exists in relationship to the other individuals whom he meets.

Thus every biography has about it one element of a confidence trick. It invites us to accept as the life-story of a human being a series of conjectures, based upon still shots cut from a film which no longer exists. It isolates the figure from the life to which he belonged. The great biographers give us a living portrait, and make us see both man and background, but only at certain moments. Of the complex a few pieces are preserved, fragments from a mosaic smashed by time, which a skilled artist has so restored and grouped as to let us guess something of the whole.

In Dover's case we run into a further difficulty. Strong character though he was, we have little direct information about him. He himself left a minimum of record. *The Ancient Physician's Legacy to his Country* and *A Treatise on Mercury*—though one has fragments of autobiography, and both are indirectly revealing—are concerned with medicine. For a knowledge of his privateering adventures we must turn to the diaries of two of his companions, in which he figures occasionally. All the time we need to use our imagination, not to invent, but to infer.

For example, there is the famous prescription, Dr. Dover's Powder. Nowadays it is not much used in this country, where its place has been taken by aspirin, but it is still much in favour on the continent. My brother-in-law, who served in Italy during the last war, informs me that he was continually being handed vast supplies captured from the Italians, and, although unable to use it in such quantities, he found it valuable in checking diarrhoea.

But apart from its basic soundness, the prescription gives us a sidelight on Dover's mind. An analgesic, it contains opium. To guard against its abuse by opium addicts, he appended ipecacuanha in proportions which made the user vomit as soon as he exceeded the proper dose. This precaution, at once neat and sardonic, suggests the sort of inference on which we shall have to depend for what we can find out about the mind that expressed itself in the extraordinary chain of actions.

Extraordinary, that is, to the modern eye. To call a man an eccentric has no meaning before there is a centre which he can be out of; before there is a recognized standard of normality. Dover and his parents and grandparents all lived in days when social change gave little opportunity for the growth of settled conventions, and people of strong character could express themselves without check from public opinion so long as they did not seriously threaten their neighbours' safety or convenience. At the same time, the very conditions which precluded settled conventions made the mass of ordinary people long for them, say so, and thus provoke the individualists into even broader gestures of self-assertion.

These gestures were all the stronger for being largely instinctive.

The aesthetic movement of the eighteen-eighties and -nineties was conscious and deliberate, a planned reaction against conventions which had had time to establish themselves. The earlier eccentrics had more red blood in their veins. They asserted, not a principle, but their own individuality. Their conduct was spontaneous, not a thought-up protest against a state of affairs of which they disapproved. Robert Dover, the Doctor's grandfather, did it is true protest against what he regarded as the decadence of country life, but the splendour and oddity of his protest raised it far above the level of a mere reaction. The protest sprang and blossomed from the essential vigour of his nature: his way of life had tougher roots than what he was opposing. Most of what he did was an effort to maintain the environment in which he could feel at home. He was trying to make his own centre in an age where there was even less agreement about a communal centre than there is today, and far less agreement as to appropriate conduct. He was not making an innovation in order to affect and startle, but trying to restore the good things of the past.

Yet although there is a clear difference between a self-conscious, often petulant protest against the way in which things are going—such as the aesthetic movement of the nineties—and the independence of behaviour which is a dynamic expression of vitality, the dividing line is not easily drawn. Graham Robertson, of blessed memory, kept out of his home at Witley all those modern devices which are designed to increase comfort and save labour. He did this deliberately, well aware of what he excluded; and, late in life, he was apt to be on the defensive against the comments no guest would dream of making. Thus, despite his integrity and genuine love of the past, his attitude was very different from that of the man who sees nothing odd in what he is doing, who cannot perhaps conceive of doing otherwise. Many so-called eccentrics have been unaware of other modes of life besides their own. Others have lived in communities so haphazard, so loosely integrated, that their oddities went unnoticed.

Among my Irish forbears was a family whose members carried intolerance of each other to such a pitch that, at dinner, each would load his plate and sit on a separate stair of the great staircase to eat it. When there was chicken, each would take nothing but a wing, a predilection which even in those lavish days complicated the task of housekeeping. No one in the family remarked on these practices, which seemed to them appropriate and normal. Only the fact that eating in solitude on the staircase happened to contravene one of the few stable conventions of the countryside, which laid down that a meal was a social occasion, aroused neighbours to remark on it, so that a report reached other branches of the clan.

These people, and many other eccentrics in Ireland and elsewhere, lived in circumstances which held nothing to inhibit their impulses. They did as they liked, and it never occurred to them to do otherwise. Above all, they were not self-conscious. Many Oxford people of middle age and over will remember W. S. Case, who abandoned a successful career in music and criticism in order to be a preparatory schoolmaster, a calling which he declared to be much better for his digestion. I once met him in the street carrying an inkpot in one hand and a cabbage in the other. He could see nothing odd in this, and was puzzled when I laughed. He wished to transport both from one place to another, and the obvious course was to carry them.

Another afternoon, when a tame jackdaw had arrived in the school grounds and had been safely captured, he caused much speculation (and some misgiving) by stopping passers-by in the street outside and enquiring whether they had lost the bird. He had at first wished to go out with a bell and cry "Oyez! Oyez!", and was only deterred by a policeman who told him he could not do this without a licence.

Once again, indignant at a recital by Madame Kirkby Lunn because the accompanist's name was not on the programme, he held up her second group of songs by walking down the aisle and pointing out the omission in ringing tones, so that the astonished singer was obliged to take her colleague by the hand and present her to the audience.

The keynote of each occasion was a complete lack of self-consciousness. Case was the perfect eccentric. His actions seemed to him entirely normal and reasonable. In the circumstances he could not imagine acting otherwise. Not until other people had expressed surprise did it strike him that there might be anything unusual in what he had done: even then he never questioned its aptness or lost confidence in it.

This unself-consciousness is the hallmark of the true eccentric. The Dovers had it, in a span of English history when eccentricity was little noted: when, in the First Gravedigger's phrase, it was not seen in them. But, before we call them eccentrics, we must be sure that we are not judging their actions in the light of today. Billy Case was a genuine eccentric because he acted, quite unconsciously, against the current of convention in his time. Actions of people in times past may seem eccentric to us now, yet have been unremarkable then, because different conventions obtained, or because there was hardly any convention to flout. Nowadays an interlude of privateering in the career of a professional man would be unthinkable. At the least, it would suggest anarchic defiance of the law. Sir William Osler fell into the trap when he wrote of "Dover the buccaneer". To Dover the expedition did not look like this at all. In his day, it was largely a matter of taking out a licence.

Still, if by the term eccentric we mean one who acts in terms of his own nature without regard to the actions or opinions of his neighbours, and whose activities seem dissociated from the pattern of his time, we may apply it to more than one member of the Dover clan. A robust individuality, uniquely expressed, emerged in the family two generations at least before Thomas set the world of medicine arguing.

TWO

ROBERT DOVER, grandfather to the doctor-privateer, left his family home in Norfolk to live at Barton-on-the-Heath, a Warwickshire village on the western edge of the Cotswolds, not far from Chipping Campden. By profession he was an attorney; by position, the local squire. With his wife Sibilla, whose father had been Dean of Lincoln, and their three children, he lived in Jacobean comfort and dignity, playing the part of hospitable country gentleman, settling the legal problems of his neighbours and resolving parochial disputes.

Even before he engaged in the course of conduct that raised him from local to national fame, Dover was exceedingly popular, having that mixture of frankness and generosity with masterful authority and a touch of the preposterous which has always gone down well in the English countryside. Once he got an idea into his head nothing could get it out. What is more, he acted upon it, vigorously and continuously, for so long as pleased him, and never dreamed of questioning either the idea or the actions into which it led him. Such single-mindedness might have got him into trouble, but his lovable qualities kept him safe, and turned it into an even greater source of popularity.

The early years of the seventeenth century were bringing changes to the English countryside, and forcing the lives of the people into new and unfamiliar forms. All country people are conservative, but these were faced with a threat to their way of life. Their boyhood warmed by the splendours of the Elizabethan summer, they felt a mean autumnal nip in the air; too harsh a contrast between "Eliza and our James".

Many of Dover's friends had watched in their teens the beacons flaring on the hilltops as the Spaniards came, had felt the quickening pulse of danger and the joys of victory. They had grown up in the high days of adventure and discovery when, meddlers apart, a man could do as he pleased: when imagination and energy and enterprise flowed in a thousand forms, when music and poetry were common speech to men of action, when the Queen could give a soldier a lock of her hair and count herself well thanked in a sonnet: when life had zest and passion, and though it could be brutal was never colourless.

Now came change. The impulse to national unity, strengthened by peril, was dissipated into faction and party. Solemnity and dullness seemed to cloud the bright individuality which they had known. The King won little love, and there were ugly doubts about his favourites; yet from this lustreless court a new code, austere, constricting, pedantic, was exhaled like a blight, threatening to kill the Elizabethan way of life with its emotional and sensuous energy, its vigorous abundance.

Robert Dover viewed this decadence with smouldering eye. Like many of his kind, before and after, he decided to his own satisfaction where the cause of the trouble lay:

> I've heard our fine refined clergy teach
> Of the Commandment, that it is a breach
> To play at any game, for gain or coin;
> And man with man their activeness to try
> Forbidden is, much harm doth come thereby.
> Mix'd dancing is a wicked horrid sin,
> And by the same much naughtiness hath been,
> That I admire to see such learning shown,
> That at our elders' churches was not known.
> Had we their faith to credit all they say
> We must believe all sports are ta'en away;
> Whereby I see instead of active things,
> What harm the same unto our nation brings.

Dover was by no means alone in diagnosing the heart of the trouble, and laying the blame upon the parsons. Thomas Randolph, the Cambridge poet, agreed with him, regarded the decay of the old country sports and games as symptomatic, and believed that all would be well again were they restored. Thus his Thenot, a shepherd boy—for some reason the poets of the time conspired to give plain English country folk classical fancy names. Even William Browne, who knew better, cluttered up his Devon lore with this ecloguery—Thenot is informed in clear, if artificial terms:

> Swain! With their sports their souls were ta'en away!
> Till then, they all were active; every day
> They exercised to wield their limbs, that now
> Are numbed to everything but flail and plough.
> Early in May up got the jolly rout,
> Called by the lark, and spread the fields about.
> One for to breathe himself would coursing be,
> From this same beech to yonder mulberry.

B

A second leapt, his supple nerves to try,
A third was practising his melody.
This a new jig was footing; others were
Busied at wrestling, or to throw the barre,
Ambitious which should bear the bell away
And kiss the nut brown lady of the May.
This stirr'd 'em up! A jolly swain was he,
Whom Reg and Susan, after victory,
Crowned with a garland they had made, be-set
With daisies, pinks and many a violet,
Cowslip and gilliflower. Rewards though small
Encourage virtue, but if none at all
Meet her, she languisheth and dies, as now,
Where worth's denied the honour of a bough.
And Thenot, this the cause I reed to be
Of such a dull and general lethargy.
Some melancholy swains about have gone
To teach all zeal their own completion.
These teach that dancing is a Jezebel,
And Barley-broth the ready way to hell.
The morrice, idols; Whitsun ales can be
But profane relics of a jubilee.
These in a zeal express how much they do
The organs hate, have silenced bag-pipes too,
And harmless May-poles, all are railed upon,
As if they were the tower of Babylon.
'Mirth not becomes them; let the saucy swain
Eat beef and bacon and go sweat again.'
And yet their sports by some controlled have been
Who think there is no mirth but what is sin.

This passage is worth quoting, despite its length and lack of distinction, because it gives a clear picture, and suggests what Dover set himself to do. Randolph was a far better writer than these lines suggest, but in one way they are entirely characteristic of him. He did not love "the Sanctified Fraternity of Black-Fryers", i.e. the Puritans. Author of a happy treatise on the merits of ale and sack, he scarcely could: but, at his best, he used laughter as his weapon rather than anger, and Mistress Flowerdew in *The Muses' Looking Glass* is softened from her rigid moralizing, to admit,

> I might have gone to hell the narrow way,

by means that would have strongly appealed to Dover.

Brooding over this state of things and on his prescription to amend it, Dover called to mind the ancient, now neglected Cotswold Games, and resolved to revive them. No sooner was the thought in his head than he was seeking means to give effect to it. He spent day after day riding around the lanes and hillsides of the surrounding country, looking for a site. At last he found it—where Gloucestershire abuts on Warwickshire, the wide unenclosed summit of a hill, with a view across the fields and cottages of Weston-sub-Edge to the trees and roofs and tower of Chipping Campden. Here, motionless, on his horse, more than seven hundred feet above the sea, he surveyed the land below, seeing already in his mind's eye the converging crowds, the competitors, the gentry, the musicians and the dancers, the jostle and bustle of it all, the trophies and the prizes. As he rode down the grassy slopes and made for home, the whole idea grew and took shape. He would have wrestling, staves, and racing. There would be horse races, greyhound races, pitching and tossing, the old songs and dances. The country folk would be roused and stirred from the monotony into which they had been allowed to drift, and the spirits of all revived in the bustle and life of the celebrations.

Dover was practical as well as imaginative, and he had a wide and varied circle of friends. Many came from the neighbouring villages and towns, and many from further afield, since his hospitable propensities made the village of Barton a pleasant place of call on a journey through the borders of Gloucestershire and Warwickshire.

Among the friends who lived near at hand, and whose business in the towns of Campden, Evesham, or Stratford would lead them close to Dover's home, were Francis Izod and John Trussell, both Warwickshire men: William Durham, Dover's godson, a young priest of Willersley who had been to school in Broadway and later became a non-conformist: John Ballard and Feriman Rutter from the nearby parishes of Weston-sub-Edge and Quenton: and William Bellas, who lived near Worcester.

It is not easy to distinguish, at this distance of time, between the friends who dated from early days and those who were attracted later by the success of the Games. Among the latter one would expect to find the men of national reputation who presently sang Robert Dover's praises; but two at least seem to have been friends of long standing. Michael Drayton, whose home at Atheston was a bare eight miles from Barton, sympathized from the first with Dover's zeal for country custom and tradition, and wrote warmly in support of his work. Thomas Heywood, another devotee of the old order, was, like Sibilla, a native of Lincolnshire, and his friendship with Dover very likely went back to their childhood. A member of the Earl of Worcester's company of players, late the Queen's, Heywood shared Dover's vigorous distaste for the Puritans.

It was probably Heywood who, when the Games were well established, introduced to the household that strange character Shackerly Marmion. The two were old friends. Marmion, a Wadham man, had further developed his vocabulary by service in the Low Countries, and been enrolled as one of the tribe of Ben, that gathering of young writers presided over by Ben Jonson. With his talent for the unseemly and his penchant for describing the brothels of Blackfriars, Marmion may well have shaken the composure of the Cotswolds when punch and late hours had loosened his tongue. Dover would think it wise, perhaps, to keep him out of the way of Sir John Mennes, fearing that, despite the range of Sir John's experience and the versatility of his talents, he might find the playwright's talk a shade disreputable for his taste— particularly if Heywood were there too to egg him on. Mennes was a remarkable survivor of the age gone by. Traveller, historian, naval architect, Admiral and Controller of the Navy, he had held a command in the Militia and served in a campaign against the Scots.

Dover's life, it is plain, was in no way bounded by parochial interests. Once the Games were established, numbers of well-known people came to the village and joined in the panegyrics to their host. There was also a constant stream of relations and connections by marriage. William Cole, Sibilla's brother, often made the journey from Lincoln. Young Thomas, studying at Oxford, wrote with affection of his "much respected uncle": and John, another of Sibilla's relations, came from the city to stretch out his shins to the blazing hearth and talk of Hyde Park and hackney coaches with the bored familiarity of the Londoner.

Thomas Sanford, who lived at Stow-in-the-Wold, had a stronger motive for visiting the house. He was soon to become Dover's son-in-law. All these and others of whom we know nothing but their names— such as Robert Griffin of Northampton—wrote in praise of their host. Some of the tributes were simple and unpretentious, some were in the form of elaborate eclogues and classical imitations, many were absurd; but all of them breathed affection and respect for Dover himself, and it is to their collective piety, as will soon appear, that we owe our knowledge of what went on and of the people who came to see it.

II

But this catalogue of friends and well-wishers has taken us far beyond the point at which Dover, riding down from his chosen hill-top, had decided to revive the Cotswold Games. The year of his resolve is uncertain. James was on the throne, the change from the old days was everywhere felt, but no clear date is recorded. All we can say for certain is that it was early in the reign, but not before 1604.

Dover was, as I have said, both practical and imaginative; and, once possessed of his plan, he went ahead with the single-minded energy of a charging bull. His first step was to extract a licence from King James, granting leave for the Games to be held every Thursday in Whitsun Week on the place that was soon to be known as Dover's Hill. Armed with the authority, he proceeded on his own account to build on the summit of the hill a portable "castle", oddly perched on a revolving stand, and depicted in a contemporary engraving with pennant flying and smoke billowing from the cannon on either side.

Dover's poet friends were delighted with this edifice:

> What Engineer, or cunning Architect,
> A Fabric of such Pomp did ere erect?

Nicholas Wallington, essaying comparisons, calls many celebrated buildings of the ancient world to his assistance, in order to give an adequate account of its splendours:

> I've heard men tell of castles in the air,
> Enchanted cells, towers, pageants most fair . . .
> Of Egypt's Pharoes' stately glasen tower
> Built by Ptolemies' magick art and power,
> Of Cheops' Pyramids, of Rhodes' Collosse,
> Of Jove's Olympic golden, ivory bosse:
> These to thy famous works compared will be
> Of small account, like them in no degree.

The engraving does its best to live up to this eulogy, but is perhaps on safer ground with its foreground portrait of Dover, to whose majestical dignity it gives full weight. Here he is helped by the special costume worn by the Founder, a suit of clothes given to him, so Antony à Wood says, by Endymion Porter, Groom of the Bedchamber:

. . . a native of that country, and a servant to that King, a person also of a most generous spirit (who) did, to encourage Dover, give him some of the King's old clothes, with a hat and feather and ruff, purposely to grace him, and consequently the solemnity.

In the engraving both costume and wearer are treated in a spirit proper to the illustrious founder of the Games. Sitting somewhat askew upon his horse, a posture chosen it may be to reveal the full splendour of his kingly garments, Dover moves with impressive dignity past the tents and the pavilions, among the galloping horses, the wrestlers, the flying javelins, the competitors leaping in mid-air or walking imperturbably upon their hands.

His presence was always the focal point of the celebrations, and he bore the honours of the occasion with a nobility which delighted the onlookers.

> Well mounted comes he there, attended on,
> By thousands of the flower of Albion:
> Grave as a Persian Sophie, his aspect
> Circled with beams of reverence, draws respect
> From each spectator. Noble Dover bright,
> Well known to all . . .

So exclaimed his friend Robert Griffin, in lines which did more credit to his heart than to his ear. There was any amount of this engaging nonsense, all manner of "panegyrick" to the Games and their high priest. John Dover, Robert's nephew, is at pains to show his classical learning. His lines contrast queerly with the robust and knickerbockered yeomen in the picture:

> Lo, where the racer mounted on a steed
> As swift as Pegasus, or a fateful reed
> Shot from a Scythian's bow, expecteth when
> The signal shall be given by certain men
> Thereto appointed, that he may begin
> His speedy race, and laboureth more to win
> The name of victor, than he doth the castle,
> Though made of silver. There the young men wrestle
> And throw the sledge, and spurn the heavy bar,
> As did the Romans in the field of war.
> In the circumference of the pop'lous ring,
> Youths intermixt with maids to memory bring
> The dancing of the ancient Druids
> And nymphs; the which, compared with these
> Would raise derision.

There is an awesome fascination about really bad verses. Even if these were not apt, I should find them hard to resist—especially the fourth line.

Horse-racing, wrestling, sledge-throwing, tossing the bar, and running the Quintain were the manly exercises in which the competitors joined. Yellow flags marked the course, guns were fired from the castle to start the races, and the winners were rewarded with a silver replica of the wooden tower: hence the allusion in the lines above.

The girls of the countryside took part in the intricate mazes and dances, and are credited, by William Cole, with leading the lines unhesitatingly to the accompaniment of bagpipe and lute:

> The country lass
> Curls her smooth tress, then looks her in the glass
> If all be right; can tell unto a hair
> How far the line will take, and whom and where.

Shepherds and country people who took no part in the Games gathered to watch the others, or to enter their hounds in competitions which have a modern ring:

> The swallow footed grey-hound hath the prize
> A silver studded collar.

Others came to follow on foot, or to watch from a good vantage point the sport of hares and hounds:

> Where beautiful horizons give
> Us shepherds leave that walk on foot,
> As long to see the leverett live,
> As he that rides with bloody boot,

—as William Basse rather ambiguously puts it.

For all who took part in the Games there were yellow favours, distributed by Dover himself as the day drew to an end, and so prized as to be "worn a twelvemonth" by the fortunate possessors. Pageant and sport were brought to an end in feasting and merrymaking, for Dover knew all about the joys of hospitality: witness Nicholas Wallington:

> When sports are ended, then appear doe free
> Token of Dover's liberality.
> His room will Xerxes army all contain,
> His tables are enfilled with guests, the plain

So ample is; so fraught and full of store,
To take ten thousand times as many more.
His drink from Wickham reaches to the hill
Runs night and day, carouse may all their fill.
He spares no cost, he also doth afford
To those that sit at any other board.
None ever hungry from these games come home,
Or ere made plaint of viands or of room.

A man of boundless goodwill, Dover seems to have had the gift of spreading his generosity of spirit to those about him. It is hard otherwise to account for the warmth of the tributes to him, many of them from men of character and wide experience of the world. There is a suggestion that his generosity told against him in his profession. D'Avenant, one of the many men of letters among his friends, wrote that, unlike most lawyers, Dover used his legal knowledge not

T'increase his neighbours' quarrels, but their joys.

This poem does not appear in the original edition of the collection in Dover's honour, though it seems to have been written at the time. It was added to the third edition (1700) and someone, probably Dover's grandson, added a footnote:

He was bred an attorney, but never tried but two causes, having always made up the difference.

Nicholas Wallington stresses his belief that the continued success of the Games, in times which were growing more and more discordant, was due almost entirely to the strength of Dover's personality:

His soldiers, though they every-one dissent
In minds and manners, yet his merriment
Ones them: Lords, Knights, Swains, Shepherds, Churles agree
To crown his sports, Discords made harmony.

Among his other virtues were conviviality, honesty, and frankness of speech:

(Thou) mayest a mirror for all lawyers be,
In thy profession for thy honesty!
It is a wonder that I ne'er could see
That creature yet, that ere spake ill of thee!

The best are glad to join thy company,
And do resort thy house most frequently.
Thy equals think it great felicity
When they but dreamed of thy society.
Inferiors like a God do thee adore
Poor wretches thine assistance do implore.
Nor young nor old, nor virgin, maid or boy,
But doth at sight of Dover gather joy.
His mirth, his games, his engines pleasing be,
To every sort of man, age, sex, degree.

"Joviall Dover", as the versifiers describe him, was the main-spring of the merriment and the inspiration of all the revels. As the years went by and the spirit of puritanism grew in power, to the men of his generation Dover became the symbol of a lost way of life. We can turn for evidence to one of the true poets who sang his praises. Ben Jonson, who had kept his head about the size and scope of the Games, eschewing classical comparisons—

I cannot bring my muse to drop her vies
Twixt Cotswold and the Olympick exercise—

spoke resonantly of their value:

. . . I can tell thee, Dover, how thy games
Renew the glory of our Blessed James;
How they do keep alive his memory
With the glad country and posterity:
How they advance true love and neighbourhood
And do both church and commonwealth the good
In spite of hypocrites who are the worst
Of subjects. Let such envy till they burst.

The creator of Zeal-of-the-Land Busy was on his home ground in the last two lines.

Michael Drayton, another to cherish affection for the glories of the past, wrote of his friend with equal warmth:

Dover, to do thee right who will not strive,
That dost, in these dull iron times revive
The Golden Age's glories; which poor we
Had not so much as dreamt on, but for thee?

> The Cotswold shepherds, as their flocks they keep,
> To put off lazy drowsiness and sleep,
> Shall sit to tell, and hear thy story told,
> That night shall come, ere they their flocks can fold.

Dover was a rare leader in an age when there were few such stalwart champions of harmless pleasures. His own explanation of the success of his scheme, put forward thirty years after its inception, is simple and modest:

> I was bold, for better recreation,
> To invent these sports to countercheck the fashion,
> And bless the troop that came our sports to see,
> With hearty thanks and friendly courtesy.

There remains only to tell how all these eulogies came to be preserved. The authors presented them to Dover, who put them away in the drawers and shelves of his library. One day an old friend, Matthew Walbancke, noticed them, and conceived a pious idea:

These flying papers coming so opportunely to my hand, I thought worthy to be published.

Dover at first frowned upon the scheme. In Walbancke's words:

His own modesty seemed somewhat adverse to have those deserved encomiums imprest.

But he gave way at last, even to the extent of adding a poem of his own, and the collection appeared in 1636. It was entitled *Annalia Dubrensia. Upon the yearly celebration of Mr. Robert Dover's Olympick Games upon the Cotswold Hills*. Several copies of this pleasant book are extant, but one example in the British Museum is of particular interest. Dover's own gift to a neighbour, Sir Thomas Trevor, Baron of the Exchequer, it bears the inscription "Robert Dover, His Presentation", and the name "Newburgh" written over the initials of one of the contributing poets. The bold strokes of this addition, and the fine deliberate signature with the rounded capital R and D, evoke the time with images of powerful clarity, till one seems to see the solid oak tables, the square, straight-backed chairs and settles, the wrought-iron fire-dogs in the open hearth, and the men who gave the scene its meaning.

Of Robert Dover the book and the signature are the only tangible things that have survived. The outbreak of Civil War shook his world to its depths, and the Games came to an abrupt stop in 1644, remote result of a catastrophe which was taking heads from shoulders and setting friends and relations at variance. We hear no more of him till 1652, when the Barton parish register records his death.

THREE

IT was the Civil War, rather than the death of Robert Dover, that put an end to this strange and most attractive chapter in English local history, of which *Annalia Dubrensia* is the monument. An absurd monument, like Dover's castle; yet built by genuine affection, and commemorating something real in the English character. It has, too, the virtues of bringing together on a lovable occasion names famous in larger contexts, and linking with them names which otherwise must have been lost for ever.

> O Time that cut'st down all
> And scarce leav'st here
> Memorial
> Of any men that were:

Here, in Herrick's phrase, is a pyramid, however odd, to keep the names of forgotten poets in our sight.

The Games themselves were revived after the Restoration, but, robbed of their centrepiece, they lost quality. A hundred years later, there was even some uncertainty as to their origin. Rudder, in his *New History of Gloucestershire*, 1779, remarks:

Mr. Robert Dover, who lived in the reign of King James the First, became a very popular man in this county by his hospitality and generosity. He instituted an annual meeting for the practice of all sorts of manly exercises, and distributed prizes to such as excelled in them. These exercises and their patron are the subject of a small collection of verses intituled *Annalia Dubrensia*, written by the best poets of that age. And there is still a meeting of young people upon Dover's Hill, about a mile from Campden, every Thursday in Whitsun Week.

It would appear that Rudder never saw the *Annalia*, or else that he was very forgetful; since on another page, in an account of Stanway Hall, he says:

The famous Dr. Dover, who instituted the Cotswold Games, died at this house in the year 1742, and was buried at his own request in the vault belonging to the Tracy family.

1742 is the date of Thomas Dover's death, not Robert's. Either Rudder did not connect Robert Dover's games with the Cotswold Games, or he forgot his former entry and followed the common practice of attaching every achievement connected with a name to its best-known bearer. Rudge, another county historian, makes the same mistake twenty-four years later:

Doctor Dover, well known for the institution of the Cotswold Games, died here in 1742, and at his own request was buried in the family vault of the Tracys.

He probably copied it from Rudder.

II

A word as to the *Annalia* themselves. The latest reprint, edited by Vyvyan in 1878, asserts that Thomas Dover issued a reprint in 1700, which contained the note "Doctor Dover thought it his Duty to perpetuate the Memory of that Good Man his Grandfather". The British Museum had six copies in all: three printed in 1636, one of which is incomplete and no longer available; one ascribed by the Museum authorities to 1700, and so catalogued; one dated 1877; and the sixth 1878. It would seem that Vyvyan either saw a complete 1700 copy elsewhere, or that he wrongly assumed the incomplete edition to be a copy of it. At all events, it includes a new poem which seems to be of the same date as the original collection, but of which the 1636 edition in the Museum shows no trace.[1]

It would be good to think that Doctor Thomas Dover felt piety towards the memory of his grandfather, but, as we shall see, the odds are that another member of the family was responsible for the 1700 reprint.

Robert Dover had four children, the eldest of whom, named after him, died in infancy. The next, John, was born in 1614, and baptized in the neighbouring village of Saintbury. John lived most if not all of his life in his native county, and, but for one short period of adventure,

---

[1] For details of the editions see Appendix A.

would seem to have spent it peacefully in the bosom of the family. His two sisters, Abigail and Sibilla, were married to young men from neighbouring parishes, and one of the weddings evidently took place before 1636, when Thomas Sanford contributed a poem in honour of his father-in-law.

John's own marriage to Elizabeth Vade, a Barton-on-the-Heath girl, must have happened some time within the next five years, since his first son, yet another Robert, died in 1642, and was buried in the churchyard of Stanway. Elizabeth's mother had come from this parish, which was to be even more closely linked with the Dover family in the future.

John, the second son, was born in 1644, by which time the peaceful life of the family had been violently disrupted. King Charles set up his banner at Nottingham, and Prince Rupert rode hither and yon throughout the Midland counties and gathered about him an army of horsemen which sorely bewildered the Parliamentary army, manœuvring slowly with pikemen and musketeers.

John Dover, now twenty-eight, joined Prince Rupert, and was made a Captain of Horse. It is reasonable to suppose that he took part in the battle fought less than twenty miles from his home, that triumph for the cavalry which so nearly brought disaster to the King. North-east of Barton-on-the-Heath, where from the brow of Edge Hill there is a commanding view of the Cotswolds, Prince Rupert's Horse were waiting for their first sight of the winding column of infantry which Essex was bringing along the London road. The attack was unexpected, and led to wild disorder. In their pursuit of the scattered militia, the cavalry were separated from the infantry. These, with King Charles in their midst, were struggling to keep hold of the royal standard until the cavalry should return to help them. By the time Prince Rupert had gathered his disordered cavalry together and returned to the charge, the standard had twice been taken, and the standard-bearer, Sir Edmund Verney, had been killed.

It is tantalizing to have no certain knowledge of these violent days in John Dover's otherwise peaceful country life. In the lulls between the battles, while the King's troops were re-forming and consolidating in Oxfordshire, he must often have returned to his home, to discuss with his father and father-in-law the movements of Prince and King, and to assess with them the strength of the Parliamentary party and the chances of a royal victory.

As the war dragged on, the troops of cavalry and foot soldiers became a familiar sight in the Cotswold villages and towns. Along the road from Bath to Newbury, from Hungerford to the battlefields at Speen and Donnington Castle, among the garrisons at Oxford and Banbury, those who served Prince Rupert professed a devotion that made them legendary. But their fortunes were on the turn. The long marches to the north, the débâcle at Marston Moor, the storming and pillaging of Leicester, the sudden surrender of Bristol: a tide of misfortune swamped them, and in the confusion which shook the land John Dover disappears from view. We do not know whether, like so many of his kind, he continued to serve the King long after hope of victory was gone; whether he spent years in forced seclusion or captivity; or whether he followed Prince Rupert into exile. The dates when his daughters were born are not recorded; but if Mary, Magdalen, Sarah, Ann, and Sibilla were younger than Thomas, the third son, or had been born within a few years of Robert and John, then the birth of Thomas in 1662, two years after the Restoration, would mean a good deal.

There is so little to go on, however, that we can hardly even conjecture what happened to John Dover. The Warwickshire Visitation of 1682 tells us that he was still alive, and puts his age at sixty-six, a figure that does not tally exactly with the baptismal register, but is near enough. There is no record of his death, nor of that of his wife Elizabeth. About her, we are told one thing only: that she was sixty-one years old when her second son, John, was born. This statement was made by Mrs. Caldwell, daughter of the said Rev. John Dover, but, especially as it would make Elizabeth older still when she bore Thomas, I can make no sense of it.

III

Still, whenever he died, John Dover had lived long enough at Shirley Farm, opposite Barton Church, to see his large family well settled and established in life. All his daughters married. Mary's husband, Samuel Hopkins, was to take part later in the same privateering expedition as her brother Thomas, and it would appear from the accounts of the voyage that he was by then in solid practice as an apothecary. Of Thomas Titford, who married Magdalen, Charles Stokes, who married Sarah, and John Leeson, who married Ann, we know nothing more than their names and where they came from. Sibilla, who was named after her grandmother, married twice. Her first husband was John Norden, her second a gentleman whose Christian

name has been omitted from the genealogical table, possibly in aston-
ishment at his surname, which was Cakebread.

John, the oldest son of the family to survive, studied either locally
or at home until 1661, when he went with a Demyship to Magdalen
College, Oxford. Here he remained for four years, but left without
taking his degree, and entered as a student at Gray's Inn. He was
called to the Bar in 1672, and then, according to Antony à Wood, he
"lived at Banbury in Oxfordshire and practised his Faculty". We next
hear of him on the roll of Gray's Inn in 1682 as a bachelor of thirty-
eight, an entry which corroborates that in the baptismal register at
Barton, "John, the sonne of John Dover Gent, baptised the 28th
October".

As a relief from his legal studies John wrote tragedies in heroic
verse, which were never acted:

... After I had read a sect or two of Lyttleton, I then to divert myself
took Caesar's commentaries, or read the lives of my Roman Generals out
of Plutarch.

One of these plays, with the provoking title of *The Roman General, or
The Distressed Ladies*, was published in 1667, and ran to a second
edition. But, even when it was relieved with these diversions, John's
heart was not in the law. In 1684 he took holy orders, and four years
later became rector of Drayton, near Banbury, where—another
tantalizing item—we are told that he was resorted to by "fanatical
people".

In view of all this legal and literary background, I incline to think
that it was this grandson of Robert Dover, rather than Thomas, who
in 1700 saw to the reprinting of the *Annalia Dubrensia*. This seems the
more likely because in the additional poem Robert's peace-making
character is favourably compared with those of the quarrelsome
lawyers in Gray's Inn, a point which would appeal to John rather than
to Thomas. The difficulty raised by Dr. Nixon, that John Dover never
proceeded to a doctor's degree, does not seem serious, since the term
"doctor" was often bestowed as a courtesy title on parsons and learned
people generally.

Another possibility is that Thomas and John got together and saw
to the job between them. I am inclined to rule this out. All the evidence
we have as to Thomas's character is that he was unlikely to collaborate
with anyone, least of all a member of his own family. He might very
well have claimed the credit, as in the note beginning "Dr. Dover . . .",

CHEAPSIDE, LONDON, IN 1740

THOMAS SYDENHAM

but the poem suggests John; and Thomas, if *he* were claiming credit for the reprint, would be unlikely to include it.

I think too that it was John who, in 1682, at the Visitation of Warwick, applied for a coat of arms and a crest, saying that they had been given as "an augmentation" to his grandfather . . . "But there must be better proof before any part of it be allowed."

The proposed coat of arms consisted of an elaborate shield surmounted by a castle and a cock, the supporters of a horse and hound, the bugle horn and cinque-foil, and the motto "Do ever good". It seems however that the application was abandoned, for we hear no more about it. The Reverend John Dover died in 1725, and was buried in Drayton churchyard.

FOUR

A PHILOSOPHER friend of mine, trained in the Brahman tradition, begins any account of himself with the words "My stock . . ." In the East, where it is claimed that not only character but special skills and aptitudes can be transmitted from father to son, so that the tenth or twentieth successive practitioner of a craft attains an intense hereditary degree of command at it, regard for ancestry is paramount: a man's stock may determine the dominant image of his life.

We in the West, while admitting the importance of ancestry and stressing it in a score of proverbs, pay it a less creative regard. Socially we have been apt to use it in order to claim privilege. As anthropologists, we have been content to note in the face of a growing child the lineaments of grandparents and great-grandparents, and to read in his character quirks or talents derived from great-uncles or distant cousins.

The data are here, but they need assembling and measuring. A doctor who diagnoses by inspecting the palms of a patient's hands described to me the constitutions and chief characteristics of my father and mother, and carried the story as far as the family of nervously unstable cousins who ate their dinner on the staircase. One member of a friend's family, so unlike the rest in talent, looks, and voice as to seem not only a sport but an apport, turned out to resemble closely an unacknowledged grandfather. A silhouette profile of my mother's grandfather as a young man might, but for hair and collar, have been taken of me at the same age; and some of my characteristics derive from his older son, my mother's uncle.

On a recent visit to a school where I was once a master, I saw the sons or nephews of nearly forty boys whom I had taught. The physical likenesses and differences were of extraordinary interest, as was all I could learn from my former colleagues about the characters of the second generation. There is a great deal to be learned, if only we knew from what premiss to start learning.

In one respect, our experience seems to differ from what is claimed in the East. Here we very seldom see inherited skill develop in crescendo.

34

With us, an opposite principle seems to work. The sons of an out-standingly gifted lawyer or doctor or actor seldom surpass him, but are either pale copies or engage in a different way of life. On the other hand, they are often better balanced and pleasanter human beings. It is as if the special energy of the father had been transmuted and generalized, so as to make him ennoble and protect normality rather than transmit abnormal gifts in a single field.

These notions become relevant now that we reach the point at which Thomas Dover emerges from his origins. John, his father, seems to have been in no way outstanding. There is no suggestion that he had anything of Robert's originality, vigour, or *panache*. John's first son to survive, the lawyer-parson, caused no disturbance either. He appears to have been a pleasant, sober, mildly-talented gentleman who read the classical authors and wrote plays for his own amusement. Thomas, John's second son, took after his grandfather, and showed much of the originality and force of character which had distinguished "joviall Dover"; but in him the mixture seems somehow to have gone awry. Energy he certainly had, but Robert's generosity and sociable warmth seem altogether to have missed him. Far from being a good mixer, he had the reputation of being short-tempered and hard to get on with, and his one broad generous gesture in giving free service to the needy seems to have lacked love and to have been made impersonally, on grounds of principle.

The one quality he drew untainted from his grandfather was that of independence in judgment and action. He had to a specialized degree Robert's power of seeing what had gone wrong. Like Robert, he over-simplified the issues, and like Robert he went bald-headed for what seemed to him the indisputable and only remedy. Both men achieved resounding success by arbitrary means, Thomas more than once; but whereas everyone applauded Robert and approved what he had done, the achievements of his grandson were saluted grudgingly, or sharply questioned and if possible denied. True, he had chosen the competitive field of medicine, where clashes of opinion are proverbial: but the chief reasons for the opposition lay in himself. He was incapable of stating his views temperately, or without abuse of those who did not share them. Nobody, in all the records, claims to have liked him.

II

On the sixth of May, 1662, Thomas Dover's baptism was recorded in the Register of Barton-on-the-Heath:

Thoma Douer filius Johanis Douer gen.
et Elizabethae uxoris ejus baptizatus sexto
die Mai An pdict.

Greater reliance can be placed on this than on the date, derived from the admission register at Gonville and Caius, which says that he was sixteen years old in 1680, the year of his matriculation at Oxford. It is stronger too, I think, than the note in the Warwick Visitation of 1682, which, giving his age as nineteen, would put his birth between the other two dates. *The Dictionary of National Biography* plumps for a still earlier date, 1660, but does not say on what authority. One hesitates to differ from a standard work, but on one or two other points the account there given is incomplete. So, with due respect, I prefer the evidence of the Church Register. In so small a place, any long delay in baptizing the child of a well-known family would be unlikely.

The first sixteen years of Thomas's life were most probably spent in Barton and round about the nearby towns and villages, with occasional visits to Banbury, Broadway, or Stow-on-the-Wold, and maybe further afield to the home of his married sisters and other relations. Like his brother John, he went to study at Oxford, matriculating on December 1st, 1680, and residing for six years as a member of St. Mary Hall, or Magdalen Hall, as it was variously called.

For the first four years he read the many authors and studied the wide range of subjects which were then the accepted preliminaries to an Arts Degree; but in 1684, after completing the statutory course and taking his B.A., he turned his attention to physic, the subject which was to bring him such notoriety in later life.

Without doubt it was his interest in medicine which took him from Oxford to Cambridge at the end of three years' further study. Very little medicine was taught at Oxford in Dover's time. Such teaching as there was ran on purely academic and theoretical lines. There were no opportunies at all for clinical study.

Thomas Dover's ambition must have accounted too for his choice of college. The Master of Gonville and Caius, Dr. Robert Brady,

Regius Professor of Physic, a staunch Royalist, had the Doctorate of Medicine conferred on him by Royal Mandate in 1660, and became a Fellow of the Royal College of Physicians twenty years later. His fame as one of the most learned Masters the College ever had must have been compensation for the long absence made necessary by his post as Physician in Ordinary to Charles II and James II.

We may be somewhat sceptical, from our modern standpoint, as to Brady's competence, since in virtue of his position he must have been one of that congeries of doctors who so bedevilled the last hours of poor Charles the Second. Be that as it may, he was well thought of in his day, and, whatever he did, it did not lose him the confidence of the next King.

In regard to his royal appointment, Venn, historian of the College, quotes an instructive estimate of his expenses:

Dr. Robert Brady, Physician in Ordinary to His Majesty, craveth allowance . . . for his riding charges and other expenses for himself, his men and horses and his attendance upon His Majesty for 144 days from 5th April to 26th August 1684, etc. . . . in all by the space of 194 days at the usual rate of 25/– by the day . . .

Brady was also a considerable historian, and Member of Parliament for the University. Whether between those avocations and his duties as physician he found any time for Thomas Dover and Co. we cannot be sure, but they probably saw as much of their Master as they expected, or as the Statutes of the time required.

The first entry of Thomas's name occurred before he came into residence. It records that he was to be admitted on the surety of a Mr. Lightwine, as a pensioner to the Scholars' table. Pensioners were roughly the equivalent of commoners today, and dined at a table of their own. Some of them, who were candidates for scholarships, dined at the Scholars' table, and it was probably on the strength of his Oxford degree that Thomas sat among the Scholars. Diplomatic relations between the two universities did not stretch as far as to make him eligible for the Bachelors' table.

There were two meals, one at noon, the other at six. The food was plain, and there were no inessential and luxurious adjuncts, such as forks. Meat and vegetables were served on pewter plates, and any extra dishes had to be paid for. Idle chatter was discouraged by the reading aloud of selected passages from a Latin bible, a duty performed by the scholars in rotation. The Master and Fellows were waited on at the high table by the Sizars, who combined the functions of students and servants, and were thus admitted to the benefits of an education otherwise inaccessible to them.

It looks as if Thomas's studies at Oxford, inadequate though the teaching was, must have helped him to some extent, since he needed only a year to gain his Bachelor's degree. After this he moved almost immediately from Cambridge to London, and went to live in Westminster, at the house of Dr. Sydenham.

III

Dr. Sydenham was a public figure of far greater stature than Dr. Brady. There was a link between them, Brady having published an open letter to Sydenham, from whom he differed upon certain medical matters. The two men differed on politics also. Sydenham, belonging to the opposite camp, began his studies at Magdalen Hall, but left Oxford when it became a Royal garrison. He served in the army, returning afterwards—in the words of Antony à Wood—"when many were ejected for their loyalty, through the interest of a very near relation": i.e. one Dr. Coxe.

In 1647 Sydenham was admitted to Wadham. He took no degree in arts, but was made Bachelor of Physic in 1648. Elected a Fellow of All Souls, where he presently became Bursar, he pursued his studies further at Montpelier, whither it seems he travelled first of all with a patient, and returned to find himself, more by chance than by design, one of the most celebrated physicians of his day.

Sydenham remained in Oxford until 1655, and many of his ideas were formed there. He was undoubtedly influenced by Cicero and by Bacon, and learned to follow Hippocrates—but he also met men of first-rate talents, who helped to clarify his attitude to life. There was Sir Thomas Clayton, Warden of Merton, and Regius Professor of Medicine; Sir William Petty, fellow of Brasenose, one of the founders of the Royal Society, an economist and a good administrator, who was also for a time Professor of Music at Gresham College; Cromwell's doctor, Dr. Jonathan Goddard; Christopher Wren; Thomas Millington, later President of the Royal College of Physicians; Robert Boyle, the philosopher; Dr. Willis; and John Locke. Of all these, perhaps he had most in common with Locke, for both men felt that observation and reflection upon what has been observed make the road which leads to knowledge.

DR. QUICKSILVER

At Montpelier Sydenham studied under Barbeyrac, who was not a recognized professor, but held extra-mural classes. Barbeyrac took pupils on his rounds, and from him Sydenham learned to base his treatment on close observation of the patient. This and his Oxford training were the foundation of a career which helped to revolutionize the study of medicine.

In 1655 Sydenham married, and moved to Westminster, where he lived in King Street. Ten years later, he moved again, this time to Pall Mall. Little is known about his wife, but he had three children.

He tried for Parliament, but was unsuccessful. In 1663 he became a Licentiate of the Royal College of Physicians—he was apparently too unorthodox ever to be accepted as a Fellow. He left London, as did many other medical men, during the plague of 1665, but this was not the dereliction of duty which on the surface it would seem to be. The practice of men like Sydenham was entirely with the well-to-do, and when these left London, as the great majority did, no practice remained there, and the doctors for their livelihood had to follow their patients to the country.

IV

In 1676 Sydenham took a Doctor's degree at Pembroke College, Cambridge, where his eldest son was studying.

In English Universities at this time, medicine was only studied as a part of a literary education. The College of Physicians encouraged medical learning, but it never occurred to any official body to encourage systematic clinical observation. It was only a handful of individual doctors who enabled advances in this field to be made.

Coming from a family of Puritans, Sydenham took his work, and his responsibility to his patients, seriously:

It is my nature to think where others read; to ask less whether the world agrees with me than whether I agree with the truth, and to hold cheap the rumours and applause of the multitude.

Though he speaks of hostility towards him in this country, he held resolutely to his own views. If physicians in England disagreed with him, at least he was followed in other countries, first by Boerhaave in Leyden, then in Vienna, in Dublin, and in America.

The hostility of which he speaks is easy to understand. Sydenham's professional attainments were the subject of much dispute among his colleagues, but the weight of medical opinion even in his lifetime was beginning to come down strongly on his side. Most of the contemporary attacks upon him arose from jealousy on account of his slender academic qualifications. We might call it trade-union criticism, a phenomenon not unknown in medical circles today. Certainly in the early days of his career Sydenham's official medical qualifications were of the slightest. Sir Richard Blackmore quoted him as an example to show that, with good sense, spirit, and address of manner, a man could reach the highest rank among physicians after a minimum of study.

This was the case of Doctor Sydenham, who became an eminent and able physician, though he never designed to take up the profession till the Civil Wars were composed; and then, being a disbanded officer, he entered upon it for a maintenance, without any learning properly preparatory for the undertaking of it.

A recommendation which Sydenham made jokingly to a young student who asked his advice, that he should read *Don Quixote*, was taken seriously by his enemies and often used against him. In this context, the remark meant that clinical observation plus the study of character would do the aspirant more good than the reading of any medical treatise. Another of his professional critics, Dr. Radcliffe, Blackmore quotes as saying that, when Sydenham died, he would leave behind him the whole mystery of physic on half a sheet of paper.

The evidence on the other side is solid and convincing. Sir Hans Sloane, who was Sydenham's pupil, strongly rebutted any suggestion that his teacher was a medical ignoramus, saying that he had never known a man of brighter natural parts. Blackmore, despite the remark quoted above, gives his practice full honour, however unorthodox the theory at the back of it.

He built all his maxims and rules of practice upon repeated observations on the nature and properties of diseases, and the power of remedies (and) has compiled so good a history of distemper, and so prevalent a method of cure, that he has improved and advanced the healing art much more than Doctor Willis, with all his curious speculations and fanciful hypotheses.

This reference to Willis's hypotheses may have been a hit at, among other things, his famous condemnation of sugar, which he held to have such deleterious effects upon those who partook of it.

Sydenham, who was the author of a great number of medical works, makes a plain statement of his own principles in the preface to his treatise *Observationes Medicae circa Morborum Acutorum Historiam et Curationem.* Here he says that he believes

that the medical Art could not be learned so certainly as by use and experience; and that he who should pay his nicest and most accurate attention to the symptoms of distempers would infallibly succeed best in searching out the true means of cure. For this reason I gave myself up entirely to this method of proceeding, perfectly confident, that while I followed nature as my guide, I could never err.

He worked always upon data gathered in his own experience, rather than upon discoveries of the past, or of other doctors. Dr. Riesman observes that Sydenham's definition of disease shows a truly remarkable insight. It is as follows: "An effort of Nature, striving with all her might to restore the patient by elimination of the morbific matter." In other words, a disease was an outsider, and all the forces of Nature within the body would fight against it. In the case of chronic disease, the body's agents reacted or developed too slowly.

Sydenham's observation was acute, and put him ahead of the other doctors of his time. For instance, a final symptom of malarial fever may be an attack of neuralgia so severe as to appear a separate disease. Sydenham realized its connection with the fever, and treated it as a part of that disease.

Following Hippocrates, he "assisted Nature" in his cures. He demanded that there should first be a description of the disease, which would give a clear picture of it.

In the second place there must be a *praxis* or *methodus medendi*, and this must be regular and exact, fixed, definite and consummate, by which I mean a line of practice which has been based and built upon a sufficient number of experiments and so proved competent to cure this or that disease. In addition to the two aforesaid desiderata in medical science a third may be enumerated, namely, the discovery of specific remedies. (*Works*, Vol. I.)

He preferred simple remedies where possible, and believed in the importance of correct food, rest, sleep, and open-air exercise.

His own health was not good, and he carried out in his own life these precepts which he advocated for others. Before he was thirty he suffered from gout, and later from calculus, haematuria, and symptoms of stone, and he was often compelled to rest from his work.

He died on December 29th, 1689, and later the College of Physicians, which had denied him complete recognition during his life, put up a tablet over his grave:

> Prope hunc locum sepultus est
> Thomas Sydenham
> Medicus in omne aevum nobilis
> Natus erat A.D. 1624
> vixit annos 65.

Where Harvey, the discoverer of the circulation of the blood, had led the intellectual and scientific approach to medicine, Thomas Sydenham, by his careful and detailed observation, had earned for himself the position of leader of its practical side.

v

Perhaps because he had not been through the mill as a young man, Sydenham stood for the rejection of dogma in scientific matters, and for a down-to-earth method based on observation. This empirical approach brought him to the forefront of his profession, and earned for him the title "the Father of Physic". By the time that Thomas Dover came to study under his supervision, he was sixty-two years old, and his practice was restricted by gout. Yet, says Dover:

he continued to increase in fame both at home and abroad, as well by his skill and judgment, as by various pieces published from time to time.

In later years, when he was working on his own medical book, Dover was frequently to refer to Sydenham's practice and teaching. In all his writing he speaks well of his old master. "Read the man whose reason was much superior to mine," he says, "the honest and good Doctor Sydenham." Dover was not the man to feign affection, and it is clear that he felt affection for Dr. Sydenham.

A much later critic, Dr. F. H. Garrison, writing in 1929, claims that in the latter half of the century (i.e. the seventeenth) internal medicine took an entirely new turn, and attributes this turn to the work of Dr. Willis and Dr. Thomas Sydenham, saying of the latter that he "ennobled the practice of Physic through his qualities of piety, good humour, and good sense".

Apart from medical teaching, Dover owed Sydenham an even more direct debt of gratitude.

Whilst I lived with Doctor Sydenham, I had myself the Small Pox, and fell ill on Twelfth Day. In the beginning I lost twenty-four ounces of blood. He gave me a vomit, but I find by experience Purging much better. I went abroad by his direction till I was blind, and then took to my bed. I had no fire allowed in my room, my windows were constantly open, my bedclothes were ordered to be no higher than my waist. He made me take twelve bottles of small beer, acidulated with spirits of vitriol, every twenty-four hours. I had of this anomalous kind to a very great degree, yet never lost my senses for one moment.

This heroic treatment brought about a complete cure. Sydenham's indifference to the possibility of spreading the infection may come as a surprise, but the fresh air and the enormous intake of liquid anticipate later treatment.

The influence of Sydenham on Dover was obviously great and beneficial. It drew added power from certain similarities of character. Sydenham's seems to have been in the round a much more amiable personality, and a more flexible mind; but his original outlook, his disregard of all his predecessors except Hippocrates, and the indifference to his contemporaries which frequently developed into open scorn, were characteristics which the younger man at once could share. From his master Dover derived many forms of treatment, such as the use of Peruvian Bark, and a demand for abundant fresh air in a sick-room, especially for consumptives.

He carried on too, and sharpened with an acerbity of his own, the tradition of despising the greater number of his fellow-practitioners and of being indifferent to their attacks. In the latter half of the seventeenth century, the profession of medicine no more conduced to mildness in controversy than to mildness in the treatment of disease. By twentieth-century standards Dover was belligerent and a fire-eater, but in comparison with many of his medical contemporaries, when they put pen to paper, he exercised a gentlemanly restraint. It is important that, without the slightest wish to tone him down, we avoid Sir William Osler's error when he called him "Dover the Buccaneer", accused him of harassing the coast of South America, and of being "thorough" in his piracy as well as in his medicine. Dover never flew the Jolly Roger; he engaged upon what his age regarded as a quite legitimate enterprise. In the same way his medical career must be looked at against its proper background, in the light of contemporary character, tradition, and manners, lest we distort and treat as fantastic a character whom his own age took seriously, and with good reason.

FIVE

AN original thinker does the ungifted rank and file of his profession grievous injury. He threatens their livelihood, damages their self-respect, and shakes their sense of security.

The majority of men are capable, at the most receptive period in their lives, of learning enough to qualify in their profession. They learn a good deal afterwards by experience, but their minds are moulded by the notions which prevailed during their novitiate, and such capacity as they have for modifying that mould and admitting other notions diminishes as they grow older. For them, everything depends on the stability of the set of notions they have learned. Anyone that attacks or questions it is a heretic, a subverter of the truth, and is hated accordingly.

This is particularly true of medicine. In no branch of science are there more rapid growth and change, more dramatic reversal of ideas. A great number of practitioners conscientiously try to keep up with all that is going on, but circumstances are against them. There is too much to learn, too little time in which to learn it. They are kept busy practising what they already know.

I do not for a moment suggest that medical knowledge is a collection of ephemeral hypotheses, and that one generation's truth is another's falsehood. Beneath each shift of ideas, each fashion in treatment, lies the broad basis of knowledge, tested and assured, which the student spends laborious years in learning. The surface of the sea looks very different in different weathers, but the water and the ocean bed remain. The truth is that scientific advances increase knowledge and improve the application of basic rules at a pace which makes it hard for the most industrious and flexible-minded practitioner to keep level.

Looming large in general practice, the problem grows acute in surgery, where it produces special reactions. Their like can be observed in many professions, but the unique power and responsibility of the surgeon make them highly important to the rest of us. The man who for years has profitably performed a certain operation is not always disposed to give three cheers for a development which means that he must painfully learn a new technique, or be superannuated and give place to a rival. Hence the conservative majority lean heavily on an inner-ring professional etiquette which helps to safeguard their interests. The phrase "trade-union criticism", which I used of Sydenham's detractors, was not meant as a term of abuse, but, quite objectively, as a label for a widely-held professional point of view which we have always with us.

At this point it may be well to make clear that I never should— or could—wish to disparage the medical profession. I owe it too much. Besides, my family is deeply involved in medicine on both sides. My two brothers-in-law are consultants, my sister is in general practice, so are a whole tribe of relatives. One cousin was Superintendent of Guy's Hospital, another Matron. I have friends in practice on the psychiatric side of medicine. There is no profession for which I have a greater respect, unless it be the allied profession of the priesthood.

This said, I may go ahead without being taken for one of those odd folk who distrust orthodox practitioners but rush to the unqualified. The fact that unqualified practitioners sometimes succeed where ordinary doctors fail is no reason for disparaging the great army of the duly qualified, who have done all in their power to learn from the best sources open to them, and to discharge a great, sometimes a cruel, responsibility.

Now let us come back to this question of the trade-union point of view. For obvious reasons, it cannot be avowed too loudly, even within the fold. If, therefore, further motives for resisting innovation can be adduced, they are welcome. Under the additional cover of patriotism —for example—many doctors have thought it more in accord with the ethics of the profession that good old A, who has been performing a certain operation for years (and belongs to the right hospital), should go on performing it, rather than let it be entrusted to B, who learned his technique abroad; even though with the new technique the patient's chance of recovery is better. The opposition to brain surgeons who were trained in America is a matter of unofficial medical history, and doctors shake their heads over it today. But this kind of thing has always been going on, in one department of medicine or another. The impassioned resistance to the principle of asepsis in surgery has had its counterpart in every generation, and, unless we have a transformation in majority ways of thought, we shall see its counterpart often in the future.

The principle which underlies all such episodes is one of history's commonplaces. The end has been lost sight of in passionate concern about the means. The welfare of the patient has been forgotten in the profession's zeal for the welfare of its members. Mediocrity has asserted itself in its own defence.

This self-protective attitude is greatly strengthened if there is any risk of an interloper enjoying the benefits without having paid the price. I was once the only layman present when four of a group of six doctors were vehemently assailing a fifth, because he had called in a specialist practitioner who had not the accepted medical qualifications—in other words, a quack—to help him with a case. The senior doctor present reviled him for unprofessional conduct. He beamed back, unruffled, blinking through his glasses.

"My dear chap, the only thing I care about is curing my patient. I'd call in the dustman if he could help. Besides, this chap really knows his stuff."

That didn't matter, the others protested. If this quack wanted to practise his unorthodox methods, let him take the trouble to qualify as they had.

The sixth doctor, a young man, spoke for the traitor.

"But—surely—the patient must come first?"

They didn't think so. This issue was between doctors only. What was important was that the patient should be treated according to the rules.

Looked at from the patient's angle (which, in his view, of course represents the true ideals of medicine), this seems grotesque, a perversion. Yet, before we exclaim too angrily, let each of us look into his heart and see if he is free of all trace of jealousy, if ever it appears that someone is waltzing effortlessly into his preserve without paying the entrance fee. When such a thing happens, it is hard not to feel something analogous to the resentment expressed by the orthodox and painstaking against the privileged latecomers in the parable of the Labourers in the Vineyard. They might at least be pardoned for losing sight of their presumed objective, the gathering of the harvest and the service of their employer.

It is bad enough to be superseded by a legitimate colleague. Even Archbishops, as Shaw pointed out, do not like being intoned off their own altars. But if the supplanter be a heretic, an infidel, a gatecrasher, someone who does not belong to the Union . . .

Any potential patient who knows many doctors, or whose work has led him among them, will hear things to make his hair stand on end. Yet no profession has higher ideals or comes nearer to realizing them in its practice. The professional's attitude to his calling will often surprise and shock the layman: it is instructive to hear ministers of religion in uninhibited conclave: but the layman is seldom in a position to judge, and never entitled to throw stones.

It will do us no harm to bear these elementary considerations in mind when we look at the state of medicine in Dover's time, and examine what he and other more distinguished doctors did to change it.

II

When Dover began to practise, medicine was emerging from a period of darkness and confusion. The old astrological foundation was discredited, and nothing positive had taken its place. No matter what may be said against astrology—and more can be said for it than later generations realized—it did at least furnish a consistent theoretical structure, a philosophy on which medical practice could be based. Once this was removed, medicine fell into a morass. It was reduced to a shapeless and obscure collection of arbitrary pronouncements and dissociated experiments which allowed the most shameless quack to flourish beside the genuine seeker after knowledge. The superstition remained, but not the underlying authority. Many of the remedies prescribed show a barely concealed belief in magic, very probably on the part of the doctor, certainly on the part of the patient.

This side of medicine has been an unconscionable time a-dying. The recipes of a white witch who practised in a Dartmoor village near my childhood home in the early years of this century were survivals from the era we are looking at. Shrewd in their mingling of tried and useful ingredients with fantastic ones, such as toads' feet, and herbs plucked in graveyards at the full moon, which were included for their supposed magical value, they could have been compounded by many a seventeenth-century doctor. They would indeed have done him credit, since most of them were likely to work quite well, even without the magical element put in to overawe the patient and keep medicine a mystery.

The honest men in Dover's day were experimenting, testing their way forward step by step. Those poets who wrote of "th'empirick Art" were unusually accurate. Lacking that body of coherent hypotheses which could establish it as a science, medicine was at its best an art, and its rules were being laid down by a process of trial and error. Yet to call a doctor an empiricist was in these days a term of abuse, much favoured by the traditionally-minded majority. Needing above all things a dogma which they could learn and transmit, they clung to arbitrary rules, many of them hangovers from astrological or magical belief.

The hard fact was that the medical men of that time had scarcely any certain knowledge. Worse, the majority took few steps to gain it. A great many doctors never saw the larger number of their patients, who were tended in their homes by apothecaries.

III

The business went something like this:

The doctor, following the current practice, goes and sits in the coffee house at certain hours in the day. To him presently comes an apothecary, and murmurs in his ear the symptoms of a patient whose case is baffling him.

The doctor ponders awhile, and rubs his chin.

"Have you tried a balm of bear's fat, assafoetida, and borax, in equal parts?"

The apothecary clicks his tongue in mortification.

"No, sir. No. It had wholly slipped my memory. I thank you."

The doctor nods benignly, and waves a hand.

"If it does not prosper, come to me again. I have a sovereign electuary. . . ."

It was to correct this sort of thing that the empirical practice of observation and the accurate reading of symptoms was developed by such men as Radcliffe, Sloane, Sydenham, Mead, and Dover, enabling medicine to progress and to benefit by the results of scientific discovery in other fields. A return towards the methodical simplicity of Hippocrates, it revolutionized both the theory and practice of medicine: and although much that these pioneers did still seems arbitrary, they had a hitherto unrecorded proportion of success, and laid strong foundations for the future.

For a start, then, let us glance at a few of the pioneers. We have already seen something of Sydenham, from whom Dover had the good luck to learn. There were others, whose work was a growing threat to the majority of their colleagues, and was therefore greeted with violent abuse. To this they reacted according to their nature. The most magnanimous took no notice. Others, Dover among them, gave as good as they got. Because of its diversity, and the ease with which unqualified or relatively unqualified men could practise, there was far

R HANS SLOANE

IN HOLBORN

Over against *Fetter-lane*, at the sign of the Last, liveth a Physitian that through Gods blessing, cureth these following diseases with honest Expedition and Concionable respect to the PATIENTS ability.

The FRENCH POX (to the cure of which there are many Pretenders, but few Performers, he cureth with Speed and Secresie, and so much ease, that they may follow their occasions, and not the nearest Relation take notice of the cure.

The ISSUE at the YARD, commonly called the *Gonorrhea*, or *Running of the Reines*, (not alwaies got by Women, as some think) he Cureth safely, and soundly, from future danger.

Consumptions.	*Pain in the Back or Limbs.*
All sorts of Feavers.	*Stoppage in the Urins.*
Pain in the Head and Stomack,	*Kings Evill. Falling sicknesse.*
Such as cannot hold their Water	*Worms. Ruptures.*
Stone in the Bladder or Kidneys.	*Rheumatick Desluctions.*
Convulsions. Rickets.	*Yellow Jaundice.*
Ptisick, or shortnesse of breath.	*Cankers, Ciatica.*
Red hair may be changed,	*Loosenesse,*
Gouts several sorts.	*Sore Eys, Freckles.*
Wind Cholick.	*Piles and Emrods.*
Sore leggs or old Ulcers.	*Obstructions of Women.*
Dropsies, as Tinpany, &c.	*Immoderate Fluxes, with many*
Barrennesse. Abortivenesse.	*others, some not convenient,*
Old Surfeits. Agues.	*others too tedious to be here in-*
Sinewes sprain'd.	*serted.*

He is to be spoken with from Two till Six in the afternoon.

"IN HOLBORN OVER AGAINST FETTER LANE . . ."

less feeling of professional solidarity then than now. Nowadays, doctors try to keep their squabbles from the public ear. In Dover's day, they slanged each other publicly, for their own advertisement. The only wonder is, when we look at the savagery of controversy prevailing in other fields, that the medical men did not use each other even worse.

IV

Dr. John Radcliffe stood on the doorstep of his house in Bloomsbury Square, sourly regarding a man who was mending the pavement.

"You rascal, you are hiding your bad work, shovelling all that earth over it."

The man straightened his back and grinned.

"Doctor, mine is not the only bad work the earth hides."

For a moment the Doctor stood glaring. Then he returned the grin, drew out his purse, and paid the man the small sum he had hoped to spare. The Doctor never changed a guinea if he could borrow a shilling, but he appreciated the thrust of a man who used the same weapons as himself.

Radcliffe, who comes to life in this quick exchange, is one of the characters who conjure up for us the spirit of the time. Their sayings and doings take us back to Thomas Dover's London, to the squares of Bloomsbury, the coffee houses in St. James, the taverns in the Strand, and make of them not a period setting, but the unnoticed environment and background of everyday life.

This is always the historian's greatest task, to revive a life for which an antique setting is the natural and only background. No amount of topographical research or description will do this as vividly as the characters themselves: men like the witty and outspoken Dr. Radcliffe, mean yet fantastically generous, who became one of the greatest patrons of learning in his time, but relied so little on it that, when he was asked where his study was, he pointed to a few phials and a skeleton and said, "Sir, this is Radcliffe's Library."

V

Born in 1650, John Radcliffe had a stormy but successful life, and made a mint of money.

"He recommended himself more by ready wit and vivacity than by

D

an extraordinary acquisition in learning," wrote Benjamin Hutchinson, his biographer. A less inhibited contemporary, when he heard the details of the Doctor's will, exclaimed that for Radcliffe to leave a Library was as if a eunuch should found a seraglio. But Radcliffe was neither ignorant nor a despiser of learning. His chief offence, in the eyes of his contemporaries, lay in ignoring orthodox medical practice and convention. "He never paid any regard to the rules universally followed, and censured them as often as he saw occasion with great freedom and acrimony." Even so, within two years of gaining his M.B. he had worked up a substantial practice in Oxford, and remained there waging continual war with the old practitioners, and quarrelling with the Rector of Lincoln, where he held a Fellowship —he resigned it rather than take Holy Orders. Then, after treating an epidemic of smallpox with spectacular success, he took his Doctorate in 1682, and moved to London. Here he established himself in Bow Street, and "in less than a year got into prime business". His wit and conversation won him many patients, his outspoken criticisms made him many enemies. He was Physician to Princess Anne of Denmark until he lost her favour by neglecting to obey her call "from . . . too great attachment to the bottle". He was constantly in attendance upon King William, whom he brought safely through a severe attack of asthma, until, in a moment of unseasonable candour, he told him that he would not have His Majesty's two legs for his three Kingdoms. His friends made efforts to have him reinstated as Royal Physician when Queen Anne succeeded her father, but she said that Dr. Radcliffe would only send her word that her ailments were nothing but the vapours; and would have nothing of his services officially.

Royal disfavour was of no great consequence to the Doctor, for it freed him from tiresome calls, which, in days of such political instability, could lead to complications. In 1686, for instance, he had excused himself from attending the confinement of Princess Anne "on account of the multiplicity of his patients—not choosing to declare himself in that critical state of his affairs".

But he carried his independence to dangerous lengths. In her last illness, he was sent for, but declined to come on the grounds that he had taken physic. This was too much, and Radcliffe was summoned before the House of Commons to be censured.

"I know the nature of attending crowned heads in their last moments too well to be fond of waiting upon them, without being sent for by a proper authority."

There was sense in his excuse, but public resentment was so extreme that he had to remain indoors for fear of assassination.

His practice, apart from the Royal Household, was large and prosperous. When he ventured five thousand pounds in an interloper bound for the West Indies with the prospect of a large return, and was presently told that the ship had been taken by the French, he was said to have replied that he had nothing to do but go up so many pairs of stairs to make himself whole again. His friend and colleague, Dr. Mead, a man of the highest medical repute, paid him high tribute, observing "He was deservedly at the head of his profession, on account of his great medical penetration and experience".

Others, both in his profession and outside it, held conflicting views. Swift, whom he treated for his dizzy spells, writes of "the caprice of that puppy, Radcliffe". Defoe sang his praises. Benjamin Hutchinson remarks that he increased in wealth and indolence to the end of his days,

. . . waging all along a perpetual war with his brethren the physicians, who never considered him in any other light than that of an active, ingenious, adventuring empiric, whom constant practice brought at length to some skill in his profession.

Be that as it may, there is no doubt that Radcliffe was a shrewd and accurate observer of symptoms, and that he turned his great earnings to noble uses. During his lifetime and in his will he was a great bene-factor to University College, and his name is doubly commemorated at Oxford in the Radcliffe Library, which he founded for the encourage-ment of learning, and the Radcliffe Infirmary, for the alleviation of pain.

VI

Robert Mead, Radcliffe's friend, was born in 1673. The son of a Non-Conformist divine, he studied medicine at Utrecht and Leyden, took his doctorate at Padua when he was twenty-two, and started a year later to practise in Stepney. The College of Physicians did not grant him a licence, but he attracted such attention with a treatise on poisons that he was elected a Fellow of the Royal Society in 1703, a year after it appeared.

Mead was one of the long and honourable line of medical men who have experimented on themselves. To substantiate his opinion that snake venom had to be injected into the bloodstream by a puncture of the fangs, he swallowed a dose and was none the worse. His learning enabled him to transmit to English medicine the Italian discovery that scabies was due to an insect. Oxford gave him his Doctorate in 1707.

In a *Discourse on the Plague,* undertaken at the request of the Secretary of State, Mead showed himself ahead of his time by insisting on the importance of preventive work and of isolating the sick. He was one of the few who recommended and practised inoculation against epidemics, and, under royal authority, used condemned criminals as guinea-pigs. Fortunately the men survived to show the value of the process.

Mead died in 1754, with no outward memorial save a mention by Pope, which shows that he was famous in his generation, both as a consultant, scholar, and patron of the arts. With an income which for many years did not fall below £5,000, he was able to indulge his tastes. His library in the Gallery of his house in Great Ormond Street contained more than ten thousand volumes, and he had exchanged many gifts of unique value with the kings of Naples and France. With all his wealth and success he remained a simple and unassuming person, honest and unfailingly generous. He valued his private gains, the *Biographia Medica* says, "as they enabled him to become more extensively useful", and never took a fee of any clergyman but one, and that to make himself even with a disagreeable patient.

VII

At a time when jealousy and virulent controversies were the accepted fashion of the medical world, only men of exceptional quality remained aloof from the scurrilities of the profession. Mead was one. Another was Sir Hans Sloane, who represents the cultured, scholarly mind of the early eighteenth century. An Irishman, Sloane at the age of sixteen suffered a haemoptosis; and the delicacy which followed may well have decided him to devote his life to medicine. In the normal course of his medical studies he passed from London to Paris and Montpelier, engrossed in anatomy and chemistry, and in the large collection of plants which was his passionate hobby. He took a post as physician in Jamaica for the opportunity of studying plant life there, and when he returned to England was chosen physician of Christ's Hospital, "applying the money received from his appointment to the relief of poor objects in the hospital, being unwilling to enrich himself by the gains he made there".

Two years older than Thomas Dover, Sloane like him had at one time lived with Sir Thomas Sydenham. The two may well have met, but their careers carried them far apart. Physician to the King, Sloane was created a Baronet by George I, and succeeded Sir Isaac Newton as President of the Royal Society. He was elected a Royal Academician in Paris, and President of the Royal College of Physicians in London. His generous benefactions to the poor, his plan for a poor people's Dispensary, his occupation with the London hospitals, his immense collection of books and antiques that were to be the nucleus of the British Museum, and the Botanic Gardens in Chelsea, were some of the public manifestations of a humane and enlightened character.

SIX

FROM that glimpse of the peaks we come to the foothills, the lowlands, and the depths of late seventeenth-century medical practice. It is important to remember that those whom we now see to have been on the peaks were not so regarded by the orthodox medical opinion of their time. In the light of that opinion they were blacklegs, knaves, charlatans, opportunists, lacking sound knowledge and therefore affecting to despise it. The pioneers we have been looking at combined originality of mind with courage to follow where it led, even though that meant incurring the enmity of most of their professional brethren.

Sydenham, Sloane, and Co. did not only stand out from a host of crooks and witch doctors: that would have made their task easy. They differed radically from men as honest as themselves, men who would have joined with them in condemning the army of charlatans further down. Once again we must remind ourselves that the profession was not nearly so well guarded as it has been since. One or two of the great ones, even, sidled into it by unorthodox means. Sydenham himself took it up as an afterthought, in order to earn a living.

Between the men of this stature and substance, and the quacks and impostors of the coffee-houses and taverns, stretched a vast range of orthodox medical proficiency and unscrupulous practice. The century had seen discovery and research in many branches of science. Anatomy, Chemistry, Mathematics, and Astronomy had made vigorous strides. Harvey's discovery of the circulation of the blood, the invention of the microscope, and other vital developments were to have tremendous effects on medicine. But in the meantime, before the discoveries had been assimilated and their significance understood, they lay open to every kind of distortion and misinterpretation, besides being a breeding ground for endless controversies of theory, refutation, and counter theory. Garrison, writing in 1929, traces many modern prejudices to the instability of the theorists in the century that followed. "It is just these eighteenth-century men who have given currency to the notion, so active in the lay mind, that the progress of medicine itself is only a succession of forgotten theories."

Even more disastrous than the disputes was the latitude which they gave to charlatans to practise upon a confused and gullible public. Popular medicine was fast returning to the excesses of the Byzantine period. There was an enormous increase in the use of bizarre and outlandish remedies: a reversal to magic.

We must not deride the magical element in medicine. Something of it remains with us today. The claims made for certain patent medicines, the deliberate obfuscation of the ignorant by the use of meaningless terms, the vociferation of vague and unverifiable statement—"Laboratory tests establish . . ." "Dentists everywhere recommend . . ." "The latest scientific experiments prove . . ." show that, even in the twentieth century, invocation will still call fools into a circle.

Not only fools. Habit and faith can play a strong part. While revising this passage, by a coincidence I came upon an apposite comment in a newspaper, which I trust that Mr. Chapman Pincher and the *Daily Express* will not mind my quoting:

You can't talk Mr. and Mrs. Patient out of using their favourite remedies—the drugs and ointments which *they* believe are the most effective for easing their aches and pains.

Medicines which were black-listed as useless by Health Ministry experts a month ago and may no longer be prescribed free under the Health Service, are now selling well in the chemists' shops.

In other words, people are willing to pay for what they believe in, rather than get something else free.

I was once lunching with a refugee psychiatrist who had practised with success in Berlin and Vienna. In London, he confessed, he found himself at a loss. His patients came for a few sessions, then unaccountably left him.

"Even this morning, there is a voman. Just as she is doing well, just as we are beginning to make progress, she goes. I cannot understand it."

I thought for a moment. Unlike the English, the Teutonic mind loves analysis for its own sake, and will pore with solemn delight over a sufficiently elaborate map of its personality problems.

"What do you tell your patients to do?" I asked him.

"*Do?*" He stared at me. "Nothing. What can they do?"

"Ah," I said. "But the English love action. If you don't tell them to *do* something, they think nothing is happening, and you're no good. This woman who wants to leave you——"

"Isn't only vanting. Leaves. Today."

"This woman who is leaving you today; where does she live?"

"Bloompsbury."

"Fine. Write and say that she has now reached a stage where you can start positive treatment. Tell her—it doesn't matter what. Tell her to get up at seven each morning, go down to Covent Garden, buy an apple, and eat it at the second lamp-post in her street as she comes back."

"But this is a nonsense! This is a magic. This is what I am never doing."

"Well, do it now—or you soon won't have any patients at all. Go on. You say she's leaving you anyway. What harm can it do?"

He was—bless him—most reluctant, but, before we parted, he promised to try.

A fortnight later, he rang me up.

"Leonard! *it vorks!*"

II

In Dover's days, when the general public knew next to nothing about medicine, and there was no smattering of scientific knowledge to make them feel superior, the magical element was immensely strong.

The London pharmacopoeias of the time contain, among other ingredients, blood, fat, bile, viscera, bones, claws, teeth, hoofs, horns; pigs' dung, cats' urine; the sexual organs, eggs, and excreta of various animals, the more unusual the better; bee-glue, cocks' combs, fur, feathers, isinglass, human sweat and placenta, the saliva of a fasting man, the hair of a menstruating woman; sponge, sea-shell, raw silk, spiders' webs, snake-skin, scorpions, swallows' nests, hedgehog spines, wood-lice—there was hardly any limit to the inventiveness shown, much of it obviously in good faith. Rich and poor alike put their faith in the extraordinary concoctions prescribed by physicians and quacks and sold by the apothecaries for extortionate prices. Proprietary medicines abounded, such as Daffy's Elixir, or Goddard's Drops, for the formula of which King Charles II gave a sum estimated to be between five hundred and one thousand five hundred pounds. Gascoyne's was a favourite powder, composed of bezoar, amber, pearls, crabs' eyes, coral, and black top of crab claw; and there were scores of others, of which Dover's alone survives—and deserved to survive.

In 1739, Joanna Steven's remedy for the stone was bought *pro bono publico* by Act of Parliament for five thousand pounds—the ingredients including egg-shell, garden snails, swines' excreta, soap, and vegetable matter such as burdock and hips and haws.

It was a widespread and lucrative trade, well publicized. Along the Strand and down the side streets of Soho signs, hung out over the passers-by, proclaimed where these pills and potions were to be had. The weekly journals carried eloquent and lurid advertisements. "Dr. Rock's infallible Liquor that cures the itch" was to be had of "the authour" at the sign of the *Hand and Face* in Water Lane, Blackfriars. A speedy cure for all sorts of agues was offered by William Deerman at the *Golden Ball*, near Hyde Park Corner—and nowhere else. St. George's shield, with a dagger in one quarter, was the trade mark of the Great Cathartick, or the Great Restorer and Preserver of Health, sold at *The Black Boy* on London Bridge.

An advertisement, accompanied by a shield emblazoned with nine large creatures, boasted that "buggs" would be infallibly cured, in accordance with a method never before published, by the undertaker, N. Sherwood, in Sugar-Loaf Court, Mark Lane. Dr. Clark, Physician and Oculist in Ordinary to King Charles II, used the *London Journal* to announce that he was now in his house in Fountain Court in the Strand, a golden head over the door, and gave weight to the advertisement with an illustration of the sun rising out of clouds and an eye radiating beams of (diagnostic?) vision, with a scroll that bore the words *"Post Nubila Phoebus"*. A. Harmer, Surgeon, was to be found at *The Golden Ball and Acorn*; Dr. Tipping at *The Cherubim's Head* in Half Moon Street, the Strand.

Dr. Godfrey chose the *County Journal* in order to advise his customers, "To prevent the Buyers being imposed upon I have put my Christian name on the top of each bottle, as in the margin". More speculative, or maybe more pious, was the assurance "Any person being most affected with any kind of ague or intermitting fever (with the help of God) I, C. Kelly, undertake to cure them in forty-eight hours at the *Golden Galleon*, three doors without Temple Bar".

"At the sign of the Anodyne Necklace" a variety of discourses and dissertations were to be found. The titles are both particular and general: on the use of Physical Necklaces for fits and children's teeth: Dr. Sydenham's observations on the Gout—this graphically illustrated: upon Noses—this book "is given gratis up one pair of stairs". Sufferers from various ailments were exhorted to buy "THE TRIPPLE PILL" from the great toy shop at the corner of Charles Street, just by Hungerford Market in the Strand; also, for a more specific disorder, "Purging Sugar Plums, the Prettiest contrived medicine for Families".

Other remedies were sold at *The Golden Ball* in Nicholas Lane, Lombard Street; at *The Hat and Feathers*, against the *Horn Tavern* in Fleet Street; at the *Rose Tavern* outside Temple Bar; and in the numerous other coffee houses and inns which were, as we have seen, the popular meeting places and consulting rooms of many of the less distinguished physicians.

III

In this hotch-potch of quackery and authenticity it must have been difficult for the initiated to distinguish between good and bad. The ignorant layman, with all the fears and superstitions of the eighteenth century to add to his bewilderment, stood no chance at all. When a tailor, William Reed, could turn oculist, attract the attention of Queen Anne by his show of opulence, and be rewarded for his services with a knighthood; when an apothecary could charge thirty shillings for a single pill, and thirty-seven pounds ten shillings for a box, and make, as Pitt attested, from one hundred and fifty to three hundred and twenty pounds on a single case; it was small wonder that quacks, greater and lesser, waxed fat and prospered. Their success did not necessarily depend on charging high fees. Some of the most famous throve on modest prices and a huge turnover. Indeed, many quacks profited from the fact that the orthodox physicians were so expensive.

John Strype, in his *Survey of London*, writing in 1726, when Dover had been in practice for many years, makes this point clear. Nobody complained, he said, about the skill of the English physicians in their profession, or about their learning in general. Whatever the public suffered at their hands was seldom due to ignorance. There was, however, a deep-seated grievance in the matter of fees. In this the doctors were like the lawyers: only the well-to-do could afford their services; "inferior people" were "undone by the exhorbitance of their fees".

An even greater hardship was due to medical etiquette. Once a physician had been called in, the patient must continue to employ him, no matter how grievously the expense bore on his resources. Once the physician had prescribed, no apothecary might do anything

to help the sick man; so that the unfortunate patient was presented
with the dilemma that he must die of the disease himself, or run the
risk of starving his family to death, if the sickness lasted more than a
week or two.

The surgeons Strype asserts to be even worse than the physicians.
Both "scorn to touch any other metal but gold"; and, as a result, the
people of London naturally fell into the hands of the quacks. The
quacks were easy of approach, their services were cheap, and lay
people had no means of judging whether they knew their job or not.
The quacks moreover had no scruples about advertising, but pointed
to lists of royal patients and "persons of great quality". This suited
their patients, who were all too ready to believe in their claims, and
who still had enough old wives' tales and superstitions, survivals from
the old magical days of medicine, to prefer remedies which were odd
in themselves, and often oddly come by.

Abuses were made worse by the rigid distinctions between the
privileges and the status of the various medical men. At the end of
the seventeenth century, the only kind to have reached a position of
any social significance were the physicians. The fashionable ones, as
has been seen, were able to make large fortunes. They were often paid
retaining fees by important or well-to-do families, which enabled them
to live in ease and comfort. Official fees, often exceeded, were half a
sovereign a visit, the equivalent of seven times as much today. These
eminent practitioners dressed with fashionable extravagance in powdered wigs, handsome coats of red silk or black velvet, short breeches,
silk stockings, and buckled shoes. Each carried, as a mark of his profession, a gold-headed cane, containing in its hollowed knob a powder
to counteract infection.

Strype, though he places them on a par with the lawyers in some
respects, says that it was difficult for them to reach the same degree of
eminence. There were fewer of them, it is true, but they were not yet
held in such popular repute as the lawyers, and, though the best of
them made almost as much money, they took a good deal longer to
make it. There was a common saying about physicians, that they
seldom got their bread until they had no teeth left to eat it.

This might or might not be looked on as an excuse for their avarice,
but it was certainly a reason for the good care they took of themselves,
and the pains they were at to avoid exertion. Here they had the advantage over the lawyers, spending the morning at the coffee houses
—when they deigned to rise from their beds—and not visiting their
patients until the afternoon. "The greatest fatigue they undergo, is the

going up forty or fifty stairs every day, for the patient is generally laid pretty near the garret that he may not be disturbed."

The physicians inevitably provoked the wit of the eighteenth-century satirists, and there are many details in the *Biographia Medica* in which one can see the seeds of the doctors portrayed by Sterne and Smollett and Congreve. Dr. Mark Akenside, for instance, settled in London, where he found himself universally admired as a poet, but remained for years unknown as a physician. His fame as a poet meant little to him, for, unlike those doctors of our own time who are anxious to excel in literature and often succeed, his whole ambition was to win distinction as a physician. Doggedly he struggled for recognition, growing poorer and poorer, and would probably have sunk altogether had it not been for the help of a friend of his, a Mr. Dyson, who financed and virtually supported him.

Akenside's *Dissertatio de Dysenteria* was commended as "an elegant specimen of Latinity", and it seems that many of the medical pamphlets written had little to recommend them but their style. There is an illuminating criticism by an unknown writer on Dr. John Armstrong's *Art of Preserving Health*. After saying (with justice) that it was very difficult to describe "gracefully and poetically" the effects of certain diseases, he calls on all readers to admire the noble felicity with which Dr. Armstrong invested his account of "the sweating sickness". "There is a classical correctness and closeness of style in this poem that are truly admirable, and the subject is raised and adorned by numerous poetical images."

Benjamin Hutchinson tells us that Dr. Peter Templeman could hardly be expected to make a success of his profession, though an erudite and liberal-minded man. He was unfortunately unable to indulge in small talk, and to follow the kind of acquaintances who were to be met with at tea tables. He could not intrigue with nurses, or toady to the various gossips and scandal-mongers whose services were so valuable in bringing a young physician to the notice of the wealthy. Instead, Templeman consorted with men of learning, or spent his leisure in serious reading.

One of the best satirical accounts was written by Bernard Mandeville, in 1730, in *A Treatise of the Hypochondriack and Hysterick Diseases*. It is worth a glance because of the point which it gives to many of Dover's sarcasms in the book which he published at the end of his life; sarcasms which might otherwise be discounted as the prejudices of a soured character.

The chief burden of Mandeville's complaint is that the training given to physicians was entirely academic. The young gentleman, secure in his knowledge of Latin, had a good time at the university of his choice. Here, in such hours as he could spare from the pursuit of pleasure, he made a gentlemanly progress through Logic, Natural Philosophy, Botany, perhaps even Chemistry and Anatomy. He then proceeded to learn by heart the names of all the diseases to which the human body was subject, and a few rough and ready signs by which one could be told from another. In the same way he learned the prognosis of typical cases, and the best things to do for them. These accomplishments being duly honoured with a degree, "which cannot be denied him", the young man was immediately consulted on the most difficult and complex cases, was ready to defend his diagnosis and treatment against all opposition, and thought himself qualified to prescribe for "the great ones of the earth".

This theoretical knowledge, Mandeville complained, was seldom supported by practical experience. There was only one way to get this experience, and most people shrank from the labour involved. It could only be acquired by continuous attendance upon sick people, a patient readiness to learn, and the capacity for unwearied and intelligent observation. "But this would not only be too laborious, but a tedious way of getting money." Rare indeed in Mandeville's day was the physician who was willing to visit the poor in their hovels, and put up with the smells and sights and squalor of a crowded hospital. The concern of the modern young physician was to get rich quickly, an ambition to which clinical observation and patience gave no support. There were quicker ways into the profession's good graces and to the confidence of wealthy patients. Let our young physician show himself a scholar or write a poem—it should be a long poem, even if it were not a good one. Let him compose a Latin oration, or even make a translation from Latin—no matter of what—and sign it with a flourish. Those unable to qualify by such means had better marry into a good family, and get their relations to help them into a practice.

Another way was to pay court to a chosen number of the most celebrated apothecaries of the day, promising them that one would prescribe abundantly of their physic, and making out prescriptions which had one important thing in common with the chimes of the Exchange, that they should be repeated every three hours. Was this too much? The young man need not give up hope. If he could gain the favour of a single wealthy man, or one with a prosperous business, he would have nothing to fear. Politics could be a help, of course. The side one chose did not matter, provided its opinions were professed with sufficient vehemence. Further professional assets were good conversation and the capacity to hold one's drink.

Finally, there was hope even for those who could not manage any of these things and were "in reality good for nothing". Such a one, provided he opened his mouth but seldom, and then only to be polite; provided he frequented a number of coffee houses in rotation, so that everybody would know where he was at any given time of the day; then, no matter how little work might come to him at the coffee houses, so long as he always took care to appear in a hurry outside them such a one would sooner or later achieve success in his profession. "Contradict nobody, never open your lips without a smile, and give no peace to your hat"—and all will be well.

Well, that is definite enough. Even though it comes from an unfriendly quarter, it has weight in conjunction with similar remarks by Sydenham, Radcliffe, and Dover.

IV

The only official medical body of any significance was the Royal College of Physicians, a Society which could trace its origins to the reign of Henry VIII. Its Statutes enacted that no man could practise Physic in London, or within seven miles of the City, without its licence; or in any part of England, unless he had taken a degree at Oxford or Cambridge. (Dover's licence from the College entitled him to practise in Westminster and for six miles round it.) The infliction of fines and terms of imprisonment on offenders, and the making of Bye-laws, were also in the College's power, and four Censors saw to the enforcement of their regulations.

Even so, these regulations were commonly evaded. Edward Chamberlayne, in his *Angliae Notitiae* (1692), pointed out that there were many physicians in London who had a good practice although they had never held a licence. This state of things was connived at by the College, which tolerated also the various quacks, the "empiricks", the wise women, and all their kind; a branch of superstition in which the English surpassed all other nations. All this was so, notwithstanding the law which made it a felony if any uncertificated person had been treating a patient who died "under his hand".

If the Royal College of Physicians, the only controlling element in the medical profession, did indeed connive at breaches of its regulations, the outlook for patients was obscure. How arbitrarily the College exercised its control can be seen from the accounts of the transactions in its own records. Medical Jurisprudence as such was unknown in England before 1788. During Dover's lifetime, and for long afterwards, the standards of the Profession depended entirely on the men who made their livings from it.

V

Next to the Physicians in social and professional status were the Apothecaries. Until the reign of James I, these had been members of the Ancient Society of Grocers. The Charter incorporating the Company of Apothecaries defined and set limits to their power. Describing the craft as a Mystery, they said that the office of those enrolled in it was to make up and prepare physic for the sick, in obedience to the prescriptions and directions given to them by the physicians. This privilege gave them the status of assistants to the physicians, "in helping men in pain and misery, and in the recovery of life and health". To deserve it, they were required to have a skilled knowledge of plants and herbs, roots and drugs, and to be qualified in the theory and practice of chemistry.

Most apothecaries were content with their subordinate status, and collaborated usefully with the physicians, saving them a lot of routine work and visiting: though this, as it prevented the physician from examining the patient, did medicine a doubtful service. Presently, however, a rivalry developed between the two branches of the profession, becoming more and more bitter as the years went by. By the end of the century, the apothecaries were turning their accumulated experience and opportunities to good account. They were constantly prescribing on their own, without recourse to the physicians, who naturally resented this diversion of fees into the pockets of their inferiors.

An anecdote from Stow's description of London shows the state of affairs that was the background of Dover's own dispute with the apothecaries. After describing the complaints made by the physicians, that the apothecaries were going beyond the terms of their office and profession, and intruding into the physicians' province by taking on themselves to administer physic directly to sick people without having the necessary knowledge, he tells us that they challenged the whole principle in a test case.

An apothecary named Rose, who had not been long in practice, had formed a valuable connection with a wealthy patient for whom he prescribed directly. The physicians proved their case in court, but the jury hesitated to bring in a verdict in their favour. As the evidence was quite clear, their hesitation threw the court into some perplexity, and the Lord Chief Justice bluntly asked them whether they did or did not believe the evidence.

After a pause, the foreman replied that the defendant had only done what other apothecaries did. On this the judge "set them right", and they brought in a verdict for the physicians.

In 1705, however, an apothecary won a test case against a physician, which had the effect of making him and his colleagues virtually practitioners, particularly among the poor. This did not improve the relations between the two sides. A pamphlet war raged, with transports of vituperation. Among those who stormed his way into the controversy was Dr. Dover.

The occasion of his entry—we have only his word for it—was the illness of a certain Miss Corbet. He alleges that the spectacular success which he had with this lady aroused the jealousy of other practitioners, and that the apothecaries joined in the row.

Another explanation is possible, but, looking at all the circumstances, we may reasonably conclude that the happy outcome of Miss Corbet's case had as much to do with the attack on Dover as had the unfortunate outcome, which he himself admits, of certain other cases.

The case of Miss Corbet attracted a great deal of attention, and, if Dover is to be believed, it became a *cause célèbre*. This unfortunate lady, suffering from a virulent attack of confluent smallpox, was seen by two physicians, one of them the celebrated Dr. Mead. They shrugged their shoulders and left the house, saying that she could not live six hours. At this point someone among her distraught relatives called in Dover, who, after a brief inspection, "desired she might instantly be blooded". Miss Corbet's mother, whom Dover describes as the Rt. Hon. the Lady Hotham, at once summoned a surgeon; but he seems to have met Mead outside, and accordingly refused, saying Mead had told him that bleeding would kill her at once. Dover was undismayed.

"Colours are all the same to the blind," he told Lady Hotham. "I have a black man who bloods very well."

Lady Hotham consented, the black man was sent for, and drew from the patient "a vast quantity of blood". Miss Corbet was able afterwards to declare that the bleeding revived her spirits, and that she felt, as it were, a new life coming on; and Dover, modestly ascribing the decision to God, records that she recovered.

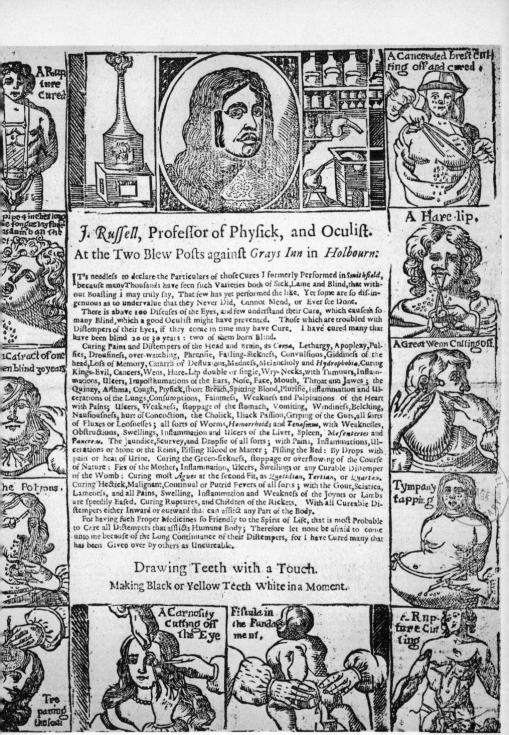

J. Ruſſell, Profeſſor of Phyſick, and Oculiſt.

At the Two Blew Poſts againſt *Grays Inn* in *Holbourn*:

IT's needleſs to declare the Particulars of thoſe Cures I formerly Performed in *Smithfield*, becauſe many Thouſands have ſeen ſuch Varieties both of Sick, Lame and Blind, that without Boaſting I may truly ſay, That few has yet performed the like. Yet ſome are ſo diſingenuous as to undervalue that they Never Did, Cannot Mend, or Ever ſee Done.

There is above 100 Diſeaſes of the Eyes, and few underſtand their Cure, which cauſeth ſo many Blind, which a good Oculiſt might have prevented. Thoſe which are troubled with Diſtempers of their Eyes, if they come in time may have Cure. I have cured many that have been blind 20 or 30 years: two of them born Blind.

Curing Pains and Diſtempers of the Head and Brain, as *Coma*, Lethargy, Apoplexy, Palſies, Drouſineſs, over-watching, Phrenſie, Falling-Sickneſs, Convulſions, Giddineſs of the head, Loſs of Memory, Catarrh or Defluxions, Madneſs, Melancholy and *Hydrophobia*. Curing Kings-Evil, Cancers, Wens, Hare-Lip double or ſingle, Wry-Necks, with Tumours, Inflammations, Ulcers, Impoſthumations of the Ears, Noſe, Face, Mouth, Throat and Jawes; the Quinzy, Aſthma, Cough, Ptyſick, ſhort Breath, Spitting Blood, Pluriſie, Inflammation and Ulcerations of the Lungs, Conſumptions, Faintneſs, Weakneſs and Palpitations of the Heart with Pains; Ulcers, Weakneſs, ſtoppage of the ſtomach, Vomiting, Windineſs, Belching, Nauſiouſneſs, hurt of Concoction, the Cholick, Iliack Paſſion, Griping of the Guts, all ſorts of Fluxes or Looſneſſes; all ſorts of Worms, *Hemorrhoids* and *Tenaſmus*, with Weakneſſes, Obſtructions, Swellings, Inflammation and Ulcers of the Liver, Spleen, *Meſenteries* and *Pancreas*. The Jaundice, Scurvey, and Dropſie of all ſorts; with Pains, Inflammations, Ulcerations or Stone of the Reins, Piſſing Blood or Matter; Piſſing the Bed: By Drops with pain or heat of Urine. Curing the Green-ſickneſs, ſtoppage or overflowing of the Courſe of Nature: Fixs of the Mother, Inflammation, Ulcers, Swellings or any Curable Diſtemper of the Womb: Curing moſt *Agues* at the ſecond Fit, as *Quotidian*, *Tertian*, or *Quartan*. Curing Hectick, Malignant, Continual or Putrid Fevers of all ſorts; with the Gout, Sciatica, Lameneſs, and all Pains, Swelling, Inflammation and Weakneſs of the Joynts or Limbs are ſpeedily Eaſed. Curing Ruptures, and Children of the Rickets. With all Cureable Diſtempers either Inward or outward that can afflict any Part of the Body.

For having ſuch Proper Medicines ſo Friendly to the Spirit of Life, that is moſt Probable to Cure all Diſtempers that afflicts Humane Body; Therefore let none be afraid to come unto me becauſe of the Long Continuance of their Diſtempers, for I have Cured many that has been Given over by others as Uncureable.

Drawing Teeth with a Touch.
Making Black or Yellow Teeth White in a Moment.

"RUSSELL, PROFESSOR OF PHYSICK . . ."

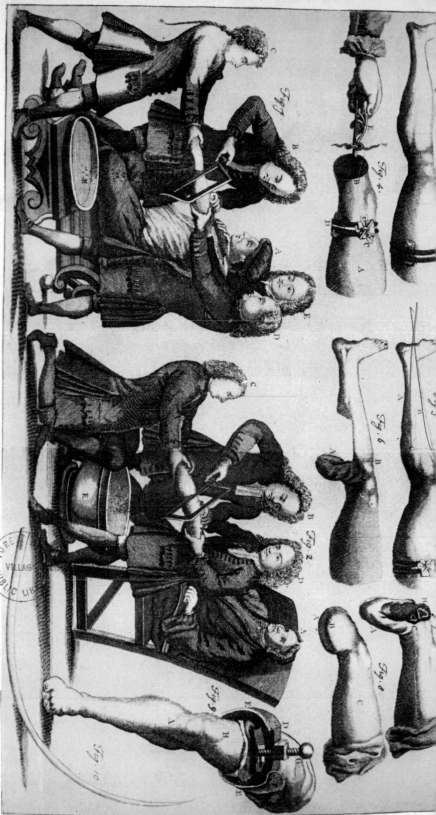

He goes on to say that her recovery was so much talked about as to occasion dismay among the medical faculty at large. It became the thing to call in Dover for desperate cases of whom their regular physicians had despaired. This was a doubtful privilege, and his way of describing it suggests that the regular physicians concerned were pleased that he had been called in, since then he might be held accountable for any deaths.

The apothecaries went one better by giving out that the death of any smallpox patient of consequence was due to the new and outlandish methods of treatment practised by Dover, whether he had in fact treated them or not. Thus, while the Rt. Hon. Louisa Berkeley and the Rt. Hon. Lady Rachel Manners, whom Dover did treat, were kept alive several days longer than anyone could reasonably have expected, the deaths of Lord Irwin, the Duke of Rutland, and "Mr. Mansel of a great Welsh family", whom Dover claimed he never saw at all, were laid at his door.

Dover protests that he never injured any apothecary, unless ordering too little physic and curing a patient too soon was in their eyes an unpardonable crime. His claim is a little disingenuous, however, since he confesses that whereas for the treatment of a fever some apothecaries could present bills of forty, fifty, or even sixty pounds, Dover's own prescriptions never earned them as much as three pounds for a single case.

"If they can't cure with less charges, I can't forbear saying, that I have the same opinion of their integrity as I have of their understanding."

The apothecaries had been having things their own way, and Dover's practice clashed sharply with theirs. There seems little doubt that he was in the right, but his manner of saying so, and the way he went about his work, only added to the injury. Many of Dover's patients, when he asked them why on earth they had not called him in sooner, told him that it was because he did not prescribe every time he visited them. This doctrine seems to be deeply rooted, persisting to our own day, when the average panel patient feels defrauded if he is not given "a bottle". In Dover's day, it was propagated by the apothecaries, who informed their patients that it was "your writing Physician only" who was entitled to a fee. The apothecaries naturally wanted a prescription, since they got the money for making it up, and their charges were high, working out at about ten or twelve shillings a time—a great deal of money, when one thinks of the difference in purchasing power between those days and ours. In any case, they were not likely to be conciliated by Dover's description of the business as picking one man's pocket to put money into another's.

What is more, Dover went on to proclaim a positive financial rivalry between the two. "The less the Apothecaries' gains are, the better the patient may afford to fee the Doctors."

It is probable that a man who wrote in this way must have spoken every bit as freely, and inflamed by his manner the resentment engendered by his practice. Characteristically, Dover maintained that all professional hostility shown to him arose from his entire devotion to the interests and welfare of his patients. This was a comfortable doctrine, and much could be made of it—including the permissible deduction that everyone who fell foul of Dover, or differed from him in any degree, was actuated by avarice and indifference to the patient's good.

VI

Next in order of legitimacy, if the term may be used when so little was legally established, came the Surgeons. These were held in low repute, and were supposed to operate only in the presence of a physician. Not until well on in the nineteenth century did surgery take its honourable place in the world of medicine. The contemptuous label "Sawbones" lasted well beyond the day of John Keats, surgeon. The seventeenth-century surgeons however were attaining a high level of dexterity, made necessary by the speed at which they had to work on patients who had no anaesthetics but drink or opium to dull their agony; and the best of them enjoyed an unwilling respect from their exalted colleagues.

Others professionally interested in the ill-health and physical processes of the English people were the Bonesetters, the Herbalists, the Midwives, and of course, the vast legion of Quacks. These Dover apparently did not think worth his shot. Tricky, astute, learned in the essentials of motive and behaviour, assessing brilliantly the limits of public credulity, they deserve a volume to themselves. They and their goings-on stretch far beyond the scope of this study, but they must be mentioned, because in Dover's day they were part of the picture. They were a part, however ignoble, of the medical profession: the cellars, so to speak, of the great edifice of medicine as it appeared to a student at the start of his career.

SEVEN

THOMAS DOVER married young, probably about the time he went to Cambridge, that is, in 1686. We do not know how or where he met his Joanna: we do not even know her surname. Her first children were twin daughters, who died in childhood. They were baptized at Barton, the Dovers' Cotswold home, in 1688, so that we may reasonably conclude this to be the year of their birth. The next child, another Sibilla, grew up safely, married one John Hunt, and had many descendants, some of whom were still living in the early years of the present century. A fourth daughter, Elizabeth, married a man called John Opie, but had no children.

In 1689 Thomas Sydenham died. Although the two men were only a short time together, he had exercised a great influence on Dover, and probably determined the course of his medical career. At the least, Sydenham confirmed him in his attitude to medicine and towards other practitioners. The best and most positive side of Dover's character owed more than we can determine to the strong-minded, sharp-tongued, kindly man whose house he had shared.

Dover admired his master, and rated him above himself as an authority. "Read the man whose Reason was much superior to mine," he exclaims, "the honest and good Dr. Sydenham." Even so, he never hesitated to disagree when his experience pointed another way.

The good Dr. Sydenham wonderfully recommends Riding in this Distemper (Consumption) . . . But, with deference to my old Friend's Judgment, I have known frequent Bleeding in small Quantities do more good than Riding.

In this he was following Sydenham's own maxim, which was to trust in observation and try, by study and experiment, to find a cure. It was the foundation, in medicine, of the scientific method, as opposed to a dogmatic teaching which had more in common with theology. Too many medical men, as we have seen, were treating traditional theories of cause and cure as revelations, instead of testing them in

67

the light of experience. Such an attitude, which regarded recovery or death alike as acts of God, encouraged a fatalism grossly out of keeping with a genuine religious approach, and Dover, a passionate individualist, who believed in God, fought it all his life.

It will not have escaped the reader that up to this point we have established next to nothing about Dover's character. Even the quotations in the last chapter came, not from the time when he was working under Sydenham, but many years afterwards, when, his work all but done, he bequeathed his conclusions to his countrymen. Facets of his character are to emerge presently, but we know precious little about him. From the fact that he got on well with Sydenham we may infer that he could command the senior doctor's liking and respect. No mean-spirited, ungenerous, or dishonest man could have stood the test of shared work and a shared home; and the quarrelsome temper which excited comment a few years later must have been under control, or found no discord to exclaim at. But that is all we can say.

To a novelist, who demands to know so much about his characters, and cannot feel confident until he sees them in the detail of their daily life, this ignorance is shocking. A novelist needs to know more about his characters than will ever appear in his story. He could tell you what any of the lesser figures did the day after it closes. Yet, here, we have hardly anything to write down about the central figure; and most of what we can write down is inference. Only at rare moments throughout the story shall we have the kind of knowledge which a novelist looks on as basic.

It is as if we were watching a huge and crowded stage, lit in patches by an uncertainly moving spotlight, and trying to follow the movements of a single figure. Most of the time we guess at what he is doing from the reactions of other characters, as they turn to look after him, or speak his name. Two or three times only do we see him, sharply lit, acting in so decisive a way as to justify all the pother made about his progress.

After Sydenham's death we know that Dover went to Bristol and set up in practice. Why he went there, what made him choose Bristol, we can only guess: but the guess is not unreasonable. Whatever else swayed him, from the point of view of his career he had made an exceedingly shrewd choice.

II

By the end of the seventeenth century, Bristol was on the way to becoming the second city in the kingdom. Its population was not large, a mere twenty-five thousand, but its natural advantages as a port and the enterprise of its merchants had won it great prosperity.

One source of its fame and revenue was dubious. It was the leading centre for the slave trade, and already, in a far from squeamish age, voices were being raised in indignation against the conditions in which the unhappy negroes were shipped to the West Indian plantations and to any other place that needed cheap labour and would pay for it.

But the slave trade was only one source of Bristol's prosperity. The merchants so seldom missed a chance of enriching themselves that they had become proverbial, and were said to sleep with one eye open. Ships crowded into King Road from all over the world, and helped to build up many a west country fortune. Inside the city walls narrow streets twisted and rambled in all directions, darkened by the over-hanging houses, and flung into tortuous angles by the sharply jutting corners. Only the main streets were paved, and these were so narrow that pedestrians had to step into doorways when they met a coach, swaying and lumbering over the uneven stones. From the open-fronted shops came all the smells and noises of a hundred trades. Tallow chandlers, soap makers, coopers, braziers, smiths, dyers, cobblers, weavers, tanners, all worked at their trades in full view of the passer-by; for each man made the goods he sold. Hardly any of the shops had glass, but used shutters and open windows, in the same way as greengrocers and fishmongers do today.

Over every doorway hung a sign; illiterate customers had no use for the printed name. They knew instead the Hand and Pen of the schoolmaster, the Sword and Crown of the cutler, and the whole host of Suns, Stars, Eyes, Sheep, Bears, Elephants, and the like that were the emblems of the various trades.

In the taverns and the coffee houses merchants did their business, lawyers and medical men gathered for their consultations. Every other day one could read the news sheets brought direct from London while one drank a penny cup of mocha, and filled one's long clay pipe with West Indian tobacco.

Folk kept early hours. Business started at five or six in the morning, the scholars of the Grammar School assembled at six, and the first meal of the day, which generally included cold meat, skimmed milk, cheese and bread, with beer or milk to drink, was taken at what we should think an impossibly early hour. By eleven or twelve the gentlemen returned home for their midday meal. The business of the day was over by five o'clock in the evening, and the last meal was eaten at six; for eight o'clock was the average bedtime, and very few stayed up after curfew at nine. There was little incentive to stay up. Tallow was costly, the streets were poorly lit and full of pitfalls, and the shutters of the taverns would have been put up long before.

Private entertaining had not yet become fashionable among the merchants, whose prosperity was displayed in their clothes, their jewellery and silver plate, and in the size and magnificence of their carriages. The wealthy men of the city, from whom the magistrates and councillors were drawn, made their money in one or other of the city's leading industries, in the distilling business, the copper refinery, in the manufacture of soap, tobacco pipes, or brass-ware, in cloth or ship-building, and—more and more of them as the years went by— in sugar refining, of which Bristol was one of the earliest and most prosperous British centres.

They enjoyed their dignity, these wealthy men, all the more for the knowledge that their city was growing to a status second only to the capital. Full of civic pride, they wore their scarlet robes at the great church festivals and the assizes, and black ones lined with fur for other occasions. They relished to the full the pomp and ceremony of the processions, the claret, the sack, and the tobacco, and the distinction which their office brought them. In many documents and records Bristol has recorded the pride which had not yet fattened into complacency. Complacency would indeed be difficult: there were still too many broils and disturbances, too many scandals and unconstitutional dealings. In 1691 customs officials and black sheep among the merchants were detected in a plan to defraud the main body of two thousand two hundred and seventy-two pounds. Bitter controversies raged among the authorities themselves. At the close of the century a plan approved by Parliament was delayed for five years by the obduracy of John Hume, the new mayor, who heartily disliked it.

This matter is worth looking into, since it was soon to involve Dover, and to give us a reference to his work from an outside source. For his first impact on the city we have only his own record. In 1695 and 1696 a "very fatal epidemical fever" attacked the city, and Dover was kept busy. For months on end he visited from twenty-five to thirty patients a day, besides "their poor children taken into the workhouse".

These last he treated free for a period of two years, not only visiting them, but paying for their medicines out of his own pocket. He did this partly out of sympathy for the children, and partly to express his support for civic charitable undertakings in general and this one in particular. There were close on two hundred of these children, and every one of them contracted a fever; but only one died.

It was about the "poor children taken into the workhouse" that the dispute arose between the old mayor and the new. A central workhouse was proposed, to be financed by pooling the Poor Rates of the various parishes. The sanction of Parliament was sought and obtained, and the plans for the new hospital were ready in 1696: but the opposition party, by every bureaucratic device available to them, so held up the proceedings that the plans could not be realized until "after our Lady-day 1698".

It would seem that Dover in his recollections telescoped two separate gestures which were greatly to his credit. Johnson, in his history of the Corporation of the Poor, affirms that

. . . The first medical man who gratuitously offered his services on behalf of the poor under the care of the guardians of the city was Dr. Thomas Dover in 1696.

This must have been a general offer, which Dover presently supplemented by the specific offer which he mentions above, to treat the children of the new workhouse. This offer is likewise in the city records, as quoted by Butcher:

The pioneer of the medical department, Dr. Thomas Dover . . . on 9th December, 1697, offered himself to be Phisitian to the New Workhouse gratis . . .

The plans for the workhouse were systematic and thorough. A building known as the Mint was taken over, and re-christened St. Peter's Hospital. A committee appointed to consider how many children could be accommodated decided on a hundred. Forty of these were to sleep in the longest room, which measured fifty feet by sixteen. The girls slept two in a bed, and were none of them expected to be tall, as each bed was five feet long and four across. The girls were to be taught carding and spinning, the "Wooll Yarn and other Materialls and necessarys" being stored in the warehouse.

Of the rooms above the warehouse the committee suggests, maybe with a touch of diffidence, that they "may be convenient lodgings for Tutors Overseers and Servants".

It would be pleasant to know how this part of the report worked out in practice. Appointments to the staff seem to have been made on a rather conservative basis. On January 19th, 1697, we read:

The Committee appointed to manage the filling the New Workhouse with poor children etc. do make the following Report vizt. That they have admitted Patience Stephens Widdow a School Mistress to teach the Children in the New Workhouse to read at the Salary of Five shillings per week the pay she formerly received of two shillings and sixpence per week out of St. Thomas Parish being taken off and that she began on Munday 17th Instant and that her rent be paid being Twelve pence per week. Also that they the said Committee have agreed with Mary Cooke the Mistress of the New Workhouse to pay her a salary of Ten pounds per annum with Diet House room washing and Lodging to commence from Michaelmas last . . .

The girls were not always suitably grateful for the pains taken for their welfare.

October 20th, 1698. The Committee appointed to manage the New Workhouse do report that they are informed by Mrs. Cook that Margaret Jones and Mary Hill two Girls belonging to the said Workhouse absented themselves from it on Munday morning last and are not yet returned and that they carryed away with them their Working Clothes and Blue Peticoats with one spare Shift and two Spare Aprons and that it is supposed they are gone for London which matter they humbly lay before this Court for their consideration Ordered that it be referred to the said committee to take care to find out the said two Girls and cause them to be brought back again if they see it convenient.

It is interesting, in view of modern practice, to see how these early philanthropists went about their job.

Our Poor's Rates we made in this manner. Every One that expected Relief came before us with their whole Families, except such as were impotent and could not come: In our Books we put down the Name of the Man, the Woman, and each Child; together with the qualifications of all, either as to Age, Health, Civility, etc. what each Person did or could get by the Week, and in what Employment. We likewise set down for what Reason the Charity was bestowed, that when that should cease, or we could find out any other way to provide for it, the Charity should likewise cease

. . . Care was taken of the various Cases and Exegencies which offered, and in all things there was regard, as much as could be, to put People on living by their own Labours.

To such as were sick, we gave Warrants to our Physician to visit them; such as wanted the Assistance of our Surgeons were directed to them, and all were Relieved till they were able to work . . .

The Committee wind up with a solid tribute to the said physician. The children flourished, since their diet was

. . . made up of such Provisions as were very wholesome, afforded good nourishment, and were not costly in price, (viz) Beef, Pease, Potatoes, Broath, Pease-porridge, Milk-porridge, Bread and cheese, good Bear, (such as we drank at our own Tables) Cabage, Carrots, Turnips, etc., in which we took the Advice of our Physician, and bought the best of every sort. They had three meals every day, and as I remember, it stood us (with Soap to wash) in about 16 pence per week for each of the One hundred Girls. We soon found the effect of their Change of living, Nature being well supported, threw out a great deal of foulness, so that we had generally Twenty down at a time, in the Measels, Small-pox, and other Distempers; but by the Care of our Physician, and the Blessing of God on his Endeavours, we never buried but Two, though we have had seldom less than One hundred in the House at any time.

Dr. Thomas Dover had his own ways of doing things; but they seem to have worked. He must also have used the method popular until quite recent times, of making his well-to-do patients pay for those he treated free; since in a very few years he was wealthy enough to indulge any whim he pleased—even such a whim as would take him away from his practice for three or four years.

The step he took argues a remarkable confidence in his ability to recover his neglected practice, or the hope of making so much money as would render him independent of it. At all events, he joined with a number of his fellow citizens in an undertaking to finance a privateering venture. The investment was highly speculative, and the dangers considerable; but, given any sort of luck, the syndicate could hope for a massive profit in the shape of prizes and plunder.

Accordingly Dover not only took a share in a pair of frigates, the *Duke* and *Duchess*, but decided to go on the expedition himself; a privateering voyage round the world.

EIGHT

IT was in 1708 that Dr. Dover laid aside the practice of medicine and embarked upon the privateering expedition which has caused so much misunderstanding and provoked Sir William Osler to set him down a rogue. The charge is an excellent example of the confusion that follows any attempt to interpret the past by the standards of the present. Although no dishonest or disreputable action is recorded of him, Dover may have been unamiable and, for all we know, one or another sort of rogue: but, by the standards of his own time, his participation in a privateering expedition was entirely respectable and earned him no reproach. At least one bishop and other church dignitaries approved the venture, and allowed their church to profit by its gains.

In fact, the expedition was planned at a highly opportune time. In that very year an Act had been passed which opened up new prospects for privateering. Its aim was to restore the old spirit of individual enterprise and adventure which had been characteristic of the reign of Elizabeth. By taxing their gains heavily, the government had discouraged privateers, with the result that the yield of the tax became negligible, and, more serious, less damage was inflicted on the country's enemies. By the Act of 1708, the Crown renounced its right to any of the proceeds. Henceforward they were to go entirely to owners and crews. Privateering was now officially encouraged, in order to annoy the enemies of the Sovereign.

Why Dover interested himself in such an enterprise is hard to say. The clear aim of those who planned and financed it was to enrich themselves. This may have been Dover's too; but he was doing very well, and to judge by the sum he contributed to the expedition's finances, he stood in no need of money. Possibly he was bored, with Bristol if not with medicine. Maybe he wished to travel, while he was still young enough to be able to enjoy the voyage, and robust enough to stand the changes of climate and the hazards of alien food and insects and disease. Scientific curiosity was probably one of his motives: he may have welcomed the chance to study tropical ailments and

74

observe the health of men on a longer voyage. Possibly he enjoyed the prospect of being addressed as Captain Dover. He may even have regarded the trip as a patriotic service, a view held or professed by some of the participants.

There must, even at the time, have been a few purists who doubted the ethics of the venture, since Woodes Rogers, the officer in command, took pains to justify it. His diary of the voyage, which he afterwards published, is prefaced by an explanation giving the official view of the whole question.

He explains that the Spaniards had from the earliest days been determined to keep a monopoly of trade with the South Seas. Both by treaty restrictions, and, where these were not enough, by force, they had prevented other nations from getting any share in it. The only channel by which English manufactured goods could come was through Spanish Factors and particular merchants at Cadiz and other Spanish ports: but these gentlemen charged such a price for their services that it was worth the while of the English and of the inhabitants of the Spanish colonies to go in for smuggling on a splendid scale. The customers encouraged the Englishmen:

As we were able to furnish them this way with better commodities and at easier rates than they had by their own galleons, not only their merchants, but even their guards did often willingly trade with us in this private manner when they could do it with safety.

"This private manner" is a happy phrase. But the traders did not stop at smuggling. Marauding attacks were encouraged, as a means to obtain the products of the Spanish possessions, and with the larger aim of weakening the Spaniards' hold on the islands and mainland of America, both North and South. King William, in 1701, laid down that "for the enlargement of navigation and commerce" the English and Dutch might lawfully seize by force what lands they could of the Spanish dominions in America, and annex them to their respective mother countries.

This was pretty drastic, even for its time: and Woodes Rogers complains that, owing to reluctance or insufficient energy, they had allowed the initiative to pass to the French, who had no such scruples. The English were therefore now in an inferior position, from which they should extricate themselves by any possible means.

Writing of the events after the expedition's return, Woodes Rogers unburdens himself. Saying that it was not for him to enquire why the provisions of the Second Grand Alliance had not been given better effect, or to decide whether a national settlement could have been made in the South Seas as soon as war began, he affirms from his own experience and knowledge that such a settlement was practicable in itself. If, in the days when he was in the South Seas, there had been a proper force to do it, the English could have settled with ease in many places, commanded provisions for their ships, and lines of communication. If the trade had been established at the beginning of the war, not only might the English have prevented the French from bringing such vast sums of money out of America, but might have brought much greater sums themselves. "Necessity has frequently put private men on noble undertakings, and I think it can't be denied that our nation is now under a necessity to make an extraordinary effort for settling a trade there."

By the end of the War of the Spanish Succession, the French had virtually ousted England from her trade with the Spanish West Indies. In other words, the piratical attacks of the French were more successful than those of the English, a state of affairs highly repugnant to Woodes Rogers and those for whom he spoke. He therefore hoped that every good Briton would approve his zeal in proposing a way to prevent "those threatening and imminent dangers", and that all would join him cordially in supporting a trade to the South Seas and other parts of the Spanish West Indies. Such a trade would of course need to be regulated officially, and would have to depend on such encouragement as the government in its wisdom had already granted, or might see fit to grant in future.

This was in 1718, long after the return of the expedition. It shows plainly the light in which these privateering expeditions were regarded. Obviously, therefore, in the eyes of his contemporaries it was no slur on Dover's character that he associated himself with one of them. On the contrary, it could be accounted to him for patriotism.

A word as to Woodes Rogers himself. His father was a sea captain, and he married the daughter of Admiral Sir William Whetstone, Commander in Chief in the West Indies, who also came from Bristol. For this, he was made a freeman of the city—"Woodes Rogers junior, Mariner, is admitted to the liberties of this city, for that he married Sarah, daughter of Sir William Whetstone, knight". He was, therefore, a man of substance and reputation, and, in the light of his experience, a worthy leader for the expedition.

II

The sponsors of this particular attempt to restore England's prestige and make a profit were some of Bristol's most prominent citizens. Among those who put down money to finance it were an ex-mayor, Sir John Hawkins; the mayor elect, John Hollidge; and Christopher Shuter, who was to be mayor two years later. Captain Philip Freake and John Clements were both Sheriffs, John Romsey was Town Clerk. Romsey, after the expedition's return, presented Bristol Cathedral with a noble pair of candlesticks, part of his share of the loot, and the Cathedral authorities accepted them with delight.

Dover himself was a citizen of good repute and standing in the town, and, as we shall see, he was treated with great respect in the dispositions drawn up for the conduct of the expedition. This respect was due partly, no doubt, to his investment in the business, but most of all to the fact that he was the only one of the leading sponsors to go on the voyage, and his fellow investors relied on him to keep an eye on things and look after their interests.

Finally—if anything further were needed to approve the expedition —Prince George of Denmark formally commissioned it, thereby giving legal sanction to what hitherto had been a private enterprise. Thus confirmed in their scheme, the organizers set about preparing two frigates, the *Duke* and *Duchess*, for their voyage round the world as men-of-war in private ownership.

III

In July 1708 the owners' representatives met together to draw up regulations for the direction and conduct of the expedition. The conclusions they came to were duly minuted and registered in the names of John Batchelor, Christopher Shuter, Thomas Goldney, and Francis Rogers. A far-seeing document, this record bears witness to the risks which anyone taking part in such a voyage in those days faced and accepted as normal. One of them, strange to our minds today, was the possibility of fatal dispute among the officers.

A plan for a voyage or any prolonged expedition is like a plan for a battle. No amount of skill or experience will enable the planners to provide for everything that happens. The most they can do is to foresee likely contingencies and decide what to do if they occur; realizing, at the same time, that many details of the plan will prove impossible to execute because of the way things will develop.

Within these limitations, the planners at Bristol did surprisingly well. Most of their anticipations were justified, and, as the records show, they at no point took too cautious or gloomy a view of what might happen when a number of men were cooped up together in conditions which gave full encouragement to jealousy, greed, alarm, and incompatibility of temper.

One of the organizers' first precautions was to define the authority and responsibility of the various officers, and lay down the proportionate share of each in the expected profits.

The command of the expedition was entrusted to Woodes Rogers, Captain of the *Duke*. Dover, in deference to his position as part owner, was to be second Captain, Captain of the Marines, and, most important, President of the Council which was to approve all decisions relating to the expedition as a whole. Moreover, because of his stake in the expedition, his share of the plunder was reckoned in thousands where others' was in hundreds.

There were to be two Councils, one on board each ship, consisting of her officers. In addition to Woodes Rogers and Dover, the leading men of the *Duke* included the pilot, Captain William Dampier, a most colourful character who deserves a biography all to himself; the owners' agent, Mr. Carleton Vanbrugh; and the Chief Lieutenant, Robert Fry.

The *Duchess*, a smaller ship—260 tons to the *Duke's* 320—was under the command of Captain Stephen Courtney. Her Second Captain was Edward Cook, her Chief Lieutenant William Shelton (or Stretton), and she was to carry the Crown Agent who accompanied the expedition, William Booth. These and at least eight other officers constituted the Council for the *Duchess*.

It was necessary to appoint two independent Councils, in case the ships should be separated: but as long as they were together they were to act as one. At the summons of Captain Rogers, Captain Dover, and Captain Courtney—"or any two of them" as the instructions ominously put it—all officers were to

. . . come aboard either ship, and be Council . . . to determine all matters and things whatsoever that may arise for the general good during the whole voyage.

All "attempts, attacks, and designs upon the enemy" were to be decided by a majority vote of the Council, and any possible dissidents were enjoined loyally to carry out the decision "cheerfully . . . indispensably and without unnecessary delay". The Council was likewise to decide all questions of discipline and to regulate

. . . any discontents, differences or misbehaviour among the officers and men, which may tend to the disturbance of good concord and government aboard either. . . .

Everyone on board, "men or persons", was to have the right of appeal to the Council through the Captain of the ship in which he sailed. These questions again were to be settled, not by the Commander, but by the vote of the majority. In the event of a tie, Dover, as President of the Council, was to have a double vote. That is to say, he could vote as an ordinary member, and add a second or casting vote in order to reach a decision.

In this particular the organizers showed either a signal lack of foresight or a dangerous ignorance of the characters of the men they were directing. To put a layman, a landlubber, in a position where he might outvote the Commander himself was to ask for trouble, unless it had been previously established that the two men were good friends and that in all instances Dover would use his second vote to support his leader. Unfortunately the President of the Council was a vivid individualist, with little feeling of *esprit de corps* or of the need to subordinate his own views to the support of discipline and the Commander's prestige. There are excuses for him. He was there as watchdog for the owners, who included himself. He had no nautical experience, and there was in those days no public school training to make a man appreciate the need for obedience to an appointed leader. What is more, one dramatic intervention of his was undoubtedly right and saved many lives. But he did not scruple to let his colleagues see his dislike and distrust of Woodes Rogers, an antipathy which the Commander most heartily returned.

There were other weaknesses in the regulations, which Woodes Rogers's experienced eye at once detected. In a note on the constitution, he complained that it gave him inadequate power to maintain discipline. Without authority to try offenders as on board an ordinary man-of-war, he found himself obliged to "connive at many disorders", and could inflict only the mildest punishments. Worse, there was no machinery or sufficient power "to determine differences among our chief officers . . . a great omission" which "might have proved of dangerous consequence".

Still, in spite of these weaknesses in the scheme, the instructions served pretty well. By and large, they worked: and it says much for all concerned with drafting them and carrying them out that, in spite of the inflammable tempers of many of the men on board, the numberless occasions for disagreement, and the hardship that beset the voyagers, the two frigates returned to port together after three whole years at sea.

IV

The first step towards equipping the ships had been, naturally, to appoint the officers. Here anyone with experience could at once detect an ominous note: there were many more than would normally be carried by ships of such tonnage. Woodes Rogers well knew the hazards of a long voyage, and enrolled the extras as a precaution against mutiny, and to allow for possible deaths among the only men on whom he could rely in times of danger.

About the officers we know little, apart from what comes out during the voyage. Most of them are names only. Samuel Hopkins, an apothecary by profession, who had married Dover's sister Mary, was appointed to assist his brother-in-law in any medical duties that might arise. Another Hopkins, William, was possibly related to Samuel, as Dover chose him for his Sergeant. His other duty was to be cook for the officers. Strangely enough, Dover did not sail in his capacity as a doctor, but took his authority as Second Captain to include supervising the health of the crews. No one seems to have had the post of official doctor, the nearest to this being John Ballot, listed as Third Mate to the *Duke*, but "designed surgeon if occasion". Ballot had plenty of experience, having sailed as doctor on a previous voyage round the world under the command of Captain Dampier.

Of William Dampier, on the other hand, we know a great deal. By the time he came on board the *Duke* as pilot, he had lived through adventures enough for half a dozen lifetimes. His professional qualifications were excellent—three voyages into the South Seas, and two round the world.

The son of a tenant farmer, he had been left an orphan at sixteen, and had sought his living at sea. After several years spent on various ships trading between English and European ports, he had served in the Dutch war, fallen ill, and come back to his home near Yeovil.

A LONDON COFFEE-HOUSE IN 1668

From an Original Picture in the British Museum.

Picture Po

CAPTAIN WILLIAM DAMPIER

Here he met the owner of a sugar plantation in Jamaica, who presently offered him the post of manager.

For a short time Dampier devoted his energies to the plantation, but he soon grew bored, and joined a ketch busied in shipping logwood. He spent two rough and hazardous years with the logwood cutters, turning pirate whenever the chance arose, and made sufficient money to return to England in 1678 with the design of settling down. He was then twenty-six years old.

But travel and the sea were in his blood. In the next thirty years he made voyage after voyage, sometimes with privateers, sometimes with pirates, and now and then under the shield of a commission from the Admiralty. He had no insular prejudice. For several years he lived with a company of French pirates in the South Seas. In 1682, and again in 1684, he cruised along the coasts of South America. On the second voyage he took his ship off from the rest on a jaunt of his own, "not from any dislike to my old Captain, but to get some knowledge of the northern parts of the continent of Mexico".

This escapade nearly cost him his life. Provisions ran short, and the crew planned a mutiny. Only the sight of land saved Dampier. His friend and colleague Swan, who had joined in the trip and faced the mutineers with him, had no doubt at all of their intentions. He looked at Dampier, who was always lean and stringy, and sighed.

"Ah, Dampier," he said, "you would have made them but a poor meal."

They put into Mindanao, and stayed there six months, most of which Dampier spent on the shore, alleging that the crew was given up entirely to debauchery, "which deterred me from going aboard, for I did ever abhor drunkenness".

Meanwhile the spirit of mutiny had got into the crew, and a section of them seized the ship, made Dampier a prisoner, and obliged him to set sail, leaving Swan and thirty-six men behind. For eighteen months he remained as Captain under duress, but argued so vociferously and maintained so stubborn and independent an attitude that, unable to bear him any longer, they marooned him with a handful of supporters on the island of Nicobar.

But the resourceful Captain had managed to secrete a pocket compass, and before long he set off with his companions in a native canoe, intending to reach some larger island in the track of shipping. The voyage was terrible. Storm after storm attacked the canoe, man after man died, till Dampier was left with only one companion. Smitten with remorse for his past way of life, which had been as disordered as its

F

circumstances, he made a resolution to amend if he should ever reach land. He did reach land, Sumatra: and returned to England twelve years after he had left, without a penny, in the company of "an Indian Prince", whom he was obliged to sell instead of exhibiting him as he intended. This "amiable savage" had only a brief experience of English life, for in a very short time he fell ill of smallpox and died at Oxford.

Dampier remained in England, writing an account of his voyage round the world, and occupying himself in divers ways until, in 1698, the Admiralty appointed him to command a ship on a mission to discover and map the islands of New Guinea. Once again he suffered shipwreck, but this time was courtmartialled and decided "not a fit person to be employed as commander of His Majesty's ships". He was moreover found guilty of hard and cruel usage.

On later voyages he was described as abusive and drunken: mutinies, desertions and maroonings were frequent among the crews who sailed with him.

His last voyage had brought him further notoriety. Alexander Selkirk, who accompanied him, was marooned; an attack on a richly laden ship bound for Manila was a failure; the *St. George*, in which he had command, was abandoned on the coast of Peru: and Dampier was for a time shut up in a Dutch prison.

For these and other reasons, after forty years at sea, Dampier was content to sail to the South Seas, no longer as Captain, but as pilot.

v

In the meantime the two ships were being fitted out at Bristol for the voyage. The crews were being collected from the taverns and eating houses, the shops and the street corners, and the owners and officers were meeting for the final arrangements. In addition to the officers already mentioned, the *Duke* carried a second and third lieutenant, a master, and two mates: a couple of young lawyers "designed to act as midshipmen": two other midshipmen: an ensign for Dover when he should go ashore: a coxswain: a boatswain and his mate: a surgeon, with mate and assistant: a gunner, with eight men for his crew: a carpenter with three assistants: a cooper with two: four quartermasters: a ship's steward: a sail-maker, an armourer, a smith: and a ship's cook.

The *Duchess* had aboard a second and third lieutenant, a master, a chief mate, four other mates, "and other inferior officers".

NINE

BY the end of July, preparations had reached a stage when the ships were nominally fit to put to sea, and the leaders of the expedition, albeit with reluctance, declared themselves ready to start. Those experienced mariners Dampier and Woodes Rogers suffered sharp misgivings, especially about the crews which they had managed to muster by methods not to be closely scrutinized. Still, the ships were three parts equipped and provisioned, however sketchily, and the manpower situation was not likely to be bettered by further delay. Moreover, as always happens, sleeping partners, the investors who were not sailing, were impatient for action. The sooner the expedition started, the sooner they might look forward to a profit.

Accordingly on August 1, 1708, the *Duke* and her consort weighed anchor, and with nine other vessels—sloops, frigates, and galleys—that had crowded together in King Road, sailed out into the Bristol Channel. Beating into a westerly breeze, they scattered along the length of the horizon, tacking to and fro until the breeze dropped at nightfall and they came to anchor off Minehead. At dawn, a shot was fired from the *Duke*, and by six o'clock the fleet sailed out into the Irish Sea. The next port of call was Cork, where the *Duke* and *Duchess* were to complete their preparations and supplement their crews.

Woodes Rogers had foreseen this last necessity, and the test of action had confirmed him. The five days spent in reaching Cork did not augur well for the success of the voyage. Indeed, twenty-four hours were enough to show the commander what he was up against, and inspire a lively entry in his log:

Our ship and the *Duchess* did not sail so well as the major part of the galleys, our masts and rigging being all unfit for sea, our ships out of trim, and everything in disorder, being very insufficiently manned; notwithstanding our number, we had not twenty sailors in the ship, and it's very little better aboard the *Duchess*; which is a discouragement, only we hope to get some good sailors at Cork.

There had been talk at Bristol of a French man-of-war cruising between the English and Irish coasts, so that hammocks were kept up and the ships cleared in readiness for a fight. A sloop which was likewise making her way to Ireland joined the fleet, but could not keep pace. The *Duchess* spied a sail, and gave chase, but after three hours lost sight of her quarry, and was glad to rejoin the other ships for the protection their company gave against the alleged French marauder. Four ships, westward bound, left the escort on August 4th, and the next day the *Duke*, in the hands of a pilot from Kinsale, first overshot the harbour, then in fog and darkness narrowly escaped turning into a bay west of Cork. This gross incompetence on the pilot's part, Woodes Rogers says, "provoked me to chastise him for undertaking to pilot a ship, when he understood his business no better".

When the *Duke* at last put into Cork, she found the other vessels had got there a day ahead of her. Here, free from interference by the owners, the two captains were able to take steps to put their ships in order. In three weeks the frigates were cleaned and tallowed, the masts were lengthened, the rigging renewed. Additional provisions were bought and stored, a number of men recruited, and the final appointments of officers made.

Woodes Rogers and Courtney were under no illusion about the crew they had engaged. The complement of the two ships numbered three hundred and thirty-three. One third of those were foreigners, and the rest mainly haymakers, tailors, pedlars, tinkers, and a fiddler or two, winding up with a negro and ten boys.

Even so, Woodes Rogers expressed himself confident that he could make an effective crew of "this mixed gang" before they had been many weeks at sea. Once they had got their sea legs and come under discipline, they could soon be taught the rudiments of seamanship and the use of arms.

Meanwhile the crew, oblivious to future ordeals, had a high old time. Expecting to sail at any moment, numbers of them hastened to get married. One, a Dane, married an Irishwoman with whom he could not exchange a word. When the time came to sail, this couple showed more grief at separation than all the rest, and the husband remained melancholy for several days at sea. The others drank happily together till the last minute, winding up with the toast to a good voyage and their own next happy meeting, and, in Woodes Rogers's phrase, "parted unconcerned".

They might not have been so lighthearted if they had known where they were going and how long they were likely to be away. A conjectured absence of three years would probably have meant mass desertions. Not till they were well at sea did Woodes Rogers think fit to make their destination known to them.

On September the first, their preparations at last completed, the *Duke* and *Duchess*, accompanied by twenty merchant ships and a man-of-war, the *Hastings*, set sail from Cork upon their various missions.

II

The man-of-war *Hastings* was under the command of Captain Paul. This gentleman showed the privateering officers the greatest consideration and kindness. On September 4th he invited Woodes Rogers, Dover, Courtney, and Vanbrugh the agent to dinner and handsomely entertained them. Well knowing the kind of voyage which lay ahead of the privateers, and the hardships they were likely to meet, Captain Paul put all his stores at their disposal; and the four officers returned to their ships with a miscellaneous load of scrubbers, iron scrapers for the ships' bottoms, a speaking trumpet, and other articles which, as he had found by questioning them, they were without. How these apparently essential articles had been forgotten at Cork no one explained.

The privateers united in praising the captain's generosity, the more so as he would accept no form of compensation, but merely asked that, when the expedition returned, the same articles should be returned to him, or replaced if lost. Next morning, Woodes Rogers, Dover, and Courtney thought it well to break to the crew where the two ships were bound, while they still had the man-of-war with them to overawe any possible malcontents. They need not have worried. Strange though it may seem, only one man objected, on the grounds that he expected to be the tithing man for his parish, and if he were not there his wife would be obliged to pay forty shillings. His objection was overruled, and he got little support from the rest of the crew, whose imaginations were inflamed at the prospect of plunder, and were calculating the fortunes they would amass in the course of a voyage round the whole world, and how they would spend it when they returned.

On the sixth the protection of the *Hastings* was withdrawn, and with many signals of thanks and expressions of hope for a prosperous voyage, the *Duke* and *Duchess* stood away and set their course for Madeira.

No ships at all were sighted until the 10th, but the captains had used the four days well, and, as Woodes Rogers had predicted, the tinkers and the tailors and the haymakers were rapidly being turned into something like seamen. The officers had used the time by holding meetings first on one ship, then on the other, laying down their plans for attack, arranging their signals, and determining their policy for the conduct of the voyage. The ships were therefore more or less in readiness when the first sail was seen, the *Duke* gave chase to her, and the days of privateering had begun.

This, the first encounter of the voyage, provided an anti-climax, but was important because it suddenly put Dover to the test and gave him a chance to show his quality. The *Duke*, much faster than the ship she was pursuing, came within range of her at three in the afternoon. Flying the Swedish flag, the intended victim turned about and bore down upon her pursuer. The *Duke* immediately fired two shots, the Swede hove to, and Woodes Rogers with a boarding party went aboard her.

The boarding party made a quick search of the cargo, looking anxiously for the contraband which they expected her to carry, and which would furnish them with a legitimate excuse for making her a prize. They found nothing, however, and, being in a hurry to reach Madeira, Woodes Rogers called the search off, and told the Swedish Master he might go on his way.

The Master, delighted, made Woodes Rogers a present of two hams and a quantity of dried beef, receiving a dozen bottles of red cider in return.

While Woodes Rogers was aboard the Swede, Dover, as second captain, was left in command of the *Duke*. Here, most unexpectedly, in this short time, he was given his first taste of mutiny. Led by the boatswain and three of the lower officers, the men demanded that the Swedish ship be made a prize. Fortunately the other officers, led by Dover, proved too many for them. Ten of the sailors were put in irons, and one, who had incited the mutiny, was soundly whipped. When Woodes Rogers came back with his hams and his beef, Dover was able to report the situation well in hand. Most of the mutineers begged for pardon, which was granted, and Woodes Rogers, in his own words, thought it safer to wink at the rest; but he instructed the chief officers to remain armed, and to keep a wary eye on the disgruntled crew.

Four days later these precautions were shown to be sound, and the captain's foresight in appointing so many officers was fully justified. With one man as their spokesman, a party numbering nearly half the ship's company came aft and demanded that the boatswain should be released from his irons.

In reply Woodes Rogers said that he wished to speak with the ring-leader alone, and went to the quarter-deck, the man, suspicious but triumphant, following him. Here the captain at once ordered the officers to seize the man, and compelled his chief aider and abetter to flog him in public. The boatswain was got rid of on the first oppor-tunity, and the mutineers, shocked by the failure of their first attempt to control the ship, went back to their normal duties and gave no more trouble.

Less than a week after this episode the two frigates, acting in unison, made their first capture of the voyage, "a small Spanish bark", and took her to Teneriffe. On board the Spaniard were four friars, one of them the Padre Guardian of the islands of Forteventura. The chief officers took an instant liking to the Padre, "a good honest old fellow". They plied him with drink, and made him "heartily merry" with toasts to the health of His Majesty King Charles II. The other three friars evidently would not join in: they were, Woodes Rogers laconically remarks, "of the wrong sort".

It makes a pleasant picture, the captors amiably disposed towards their captives, and the old friar, who probably understood little if anything of the toasts he was drinking, accepting drink and fellowship as naturally as he had accepted capture. His sour-faced brothers in God may have had bitter things to say to him afterwards; but his attitude, with its uncomplaining acceptance of whatever life might bring—like the cheerful fatalism of the crew when told that they would probably be three years from home—must have been almost a condition of survival in an age when so much in life was uncertain. To us, little safeguarded though we may think ourselves, such happy-go-lucky readiness to take life as it comes is hard to believe. It would seem harder still, had not the years of war taught us how quickly we learned to tolerate a continuous degree of uncertainty which, when we look back on it, appears intolerable.

The object of putting into Teneriffe was to obtain ransom for the prize. Here the expedition met with an unexpected obstacle, due, at least in part, to the impetuosity and stubbornness of Mr. Vanbrugh. The agent, relying on his position as the owners' representative, felt entitled to act without consulting his commander, and went ashore on his own responsibility. He looked on the matter as a business trans-action, falling within his province, not Woodes Rogers's, and was fully confident in his ability to get a good price for the Spanish ship. Part of the money he planned, very properly, to spend on fresh provisions.

The Island authorities saw otherwise. They protested that the

Spanish ship was fully within her rights, her trade having been made legal by an agreement with Her Britannic Majesty. Accordingly they demanded that the prize be at once surrendered, and held the indignant Vanbrugh as a hostage until Woodes Rogers should hand her over.

A council of war was held at once and returned a decisive answer. The English captains did not seek trouble, but would not be imposed upon. They had no intention of honouring an agreement about which they had never been informed. As for Mr. Vanbrugh, it was his misfortune to go on shore, "and if he is detained, we can't help it". Not only would they hold fast to the prize and keep the prisoners, but, if their terms of ransom were not accepted, they would draw close inshore and use their guns to fire the town. This was an ultimatum: the islanders had a few hours in which to make up their minds.

In fact, Woodes Rogers, Dover and Co. were nowhere near as confident as their words proclaimed. They had heard that several French men-of-war were expected to call in at the island, and kept an uneasy eye lifting for their approach. Happily, however, the bluff worked. As the hour named in the ultimatum approached, a boat put out from shore, in which was presently discerned Mr. Vanbrugh, sitting in the stern and presiding over a miscellaneous cargo of wine, fruit, hogs, and vegetables. As the boat drew alongside, he wore, not the smile of the victor, but the grim-jawed glare of one determined to make things hot for the shipmates who had been ready to leave him behind.

He lost no time in lodging his protest, but found a united council against him. All felt that he had taken too much upon himself, and was wholly to blame for what he had suffered. A vote was taken, registering the Council's judgment that "Mr. Vanbrugh had been much in the wrong, and that he and no other was to be censured".

Woodes Rogers, doubtless with an eye to the powers whom Vanbrugh represented, referred very temperately to the affair—"Mr. Vanbrugh complained that I had not treated him as I ought"—and left the minutes of the Council to convince subsequent enquirers where the blame lay.

In the event, discord was resolved. The exchange of provisions was completed to the satisfaction of all concerned, the prisoners were all set free, Mr. Vanbrugh swallowed his chagrin, and the Council set their seal upon the transaction by presenting the Padre Guardian, who had retained their affection throughout the negotiations, with a handsome cheese.

III

For the next few days the voyage was continued without incident. On September 25th the frigates crossed the line, and the customary ducking was administered to those whose first time it was.

The manner of doing it was by a rope through a block to the mainyard, to hoist 'em above half way up to the yard and let fall at once into the water; and having a stick cross through their legs and well fastened to the rope so that they might not be surprised and let go their hold.

Those who preferred to avoid the ducking could get off by paying half-a-crown into a fund to be spent on entertaining the ship's company when they got back to England. Half-a-crown was a lot of money in those days, and the great majority preferred the ducking, with its attendant fun and horseplay.

The week that followed brought the first casualty. A sailor at work on the maintop suddenly fell overboard without a cry and disappeared. There was no question of rescue, and no chance for Dover to find out what was wrong with him. The general theory was that he had had an epileptic fit.

On the last day of the month, both ships came to anchor in the bay of St. Vincent. The immediate purpose was to provision them for the long Atlantic crossing to Brazil, and especially to take in fresh water. Woodes Rogers seized the opportunity to burn the water-casks clean. They had once contained oil, "and for want of cleaning made the water stink insufferably".

A disadvantage of this interlude was that the men had to be allowed on shore, where their hard-won discipline was immediately relaxed. Once off the ships, no argument or remonstrance could stop them from bartering their clothing to the natives for any sort of goods that took their fancy. Ignorant, lulled by the tropical warmth, they would not listen to talk of South Atlantic gales; and the officers were left ruefully to make such provisions as they could for defending them against the bitter weather that lay ahead. Limes, tobacco, oranges, fowls, potatoes, hogs, "bananoes", musk, water-melons, and brandy were loaded into the ships, and at the last moment, "two good black cattle": but these transactions cost the expedition its second loss. They had sent ashore a man who knew the language, and entrusted him with the initial arrangements. "The Linguist" did his job well, but failed to show up when it was concluded. The council waited a day or so, then concluded that he was lost or had deserted, and sailed southward without him.

IV

Thus the first stage of the expedition had passed without serious mishap, and without any outbreak of the discord which was soon to mar the relationship between Dover and Woodes Rogers. The dangers of the position, with the inexperienced landsman promoted to all but equal status because he was part owner, must have been clear to both men from the start. They were not naturally suited to be friends, and that too must have been clear to them. There was all the more reason, therefore, for each to go carefully and avoid giving the other cause for offence.

This policy they both followed, and were helped by the turn of events. The first outbreak of disorder, when Woodes Rogers was aboard the Spanish ship, Dover dealt with in a manner which earned the commander's respect. Here was a man who, landlubber though he was, would stand no nonsense. And Woodes Rogers, by approving what his Second Captain had done, and continuing the same policy, won Dover's respect in return.

The intransigence of Vanbrugh made a further bond, and, since Dover was one of the owners whom the agent represented, Woodes Rogers must have been especially grateful to find him in agreement with his own view of Vanbrugh's behaviour. So far, so good; but the concord was too good to last. The strain of living at close quarters for months and years can breed quarrels between people who like each other, let alone men who have little besides strength of character in common.

Before we go any further, I had better establish our authority for the chapters that follow.

There are two main sources of information about the voyage of the Bristol privateers: the journals kept by Captain Woodes Rogers and Captain Cooke. Cooke's appeared first in 1712; Woodes Rogers's in 1718—chiefly, he tells us, as a defence against attacks upon his reputation by certain following voyagers.

Of the two, Woodes Rogers's is by far the livelier, and shows far more concern with the personal relationships of those on board. Where both men describe the same incident, Woodes Rogers's account is nearly always the more graphic and vivid. I have therefore based the chapters that follow on his account, using Cooke's to check its accuracy, except on the few occasions when a paragraph or a sentence springs to life on his page.

This Morass Ground (at Guaiaquil) was full of the largest Toads I ever saw, some of them as big as an English Twopenny loaf. . . .

Not that Cooke's Journal is negligible, or inferior. In some respects he has the advantage. A man of wide knowledge, with a robustly practical cast of mind, he is far stronger on the historical and geographical aspects of the voyage than Woodes Rogers. In language that is often terse and technical, Cooke lists signals by day, by night, in a fog, and for line of battle. He gives wind directions, particulars of latitude and longitude, charts and maps, and a great many drawings of birds and fish seen on the voyage. Much more than a journal, his book offers the reader a comprehensive view of the places the frigates touched on during the voyage, with their historical background, and detailed descriptions of the people and their habits and customs. His general curiosity was much wider than Woodes Rogers's, but he lays far less stress on personal feelings, and has much less to say about the characters of officers and men; a want which makes him less valuable for our present purpose.

I shall quote from him where he has something to add, and here and there the story of an episode will be a composite of the two accounts: but the greater part will derive from Woodes Rogers.

TEN

O N the 8th October the two frigates put in at one of the Cape Verde Islands. Short though the interval at sea had been, officers and crews were glad of the chance to go ashore and get fresh food. On shore they fell in with a small band of negroes from St. Nicholas and St. Antonia, who had come there in search of turtle, the oil of which was highly prized in their communities. The turtle apparently reached their best at this season of the year, and the negroes declared that they made excellent eating. Woodes Rogers accepted the recommendation—within limits. He does not say whether Dover or any of the other medical officers prompted his caution, but, though he procured a number of turtles, he reserved them for the crew.

Encouraged by the reports of the islanders, shore parties decided to go hunting. There were a few wild goats, plenty of wild asses, and any amount of guinea-hens, curlews, and sea fowls. Killing the birds was easy enough, but the huntsmen had no larger success. The only game they startled was a wild ass, which led them a protracted dance. They managed to get in a shot, and claimed to have hit him, but his pace was too much for them. They returned, angry and empty-handed, complaining bitterly of spiders whose webs, stretched between the trees, were so strong that a man had a struggle to get through them.

Sailing on, and getting their first sight of flying fish, the frigates struck bad weather, which did not clear till the 22nd of the month. The weather seems to have had its effect upon the tempers of the voyagers. As the result of a dispute, the two captains decided to exchange the second mate of the *Duchess*, whose name was Page, for his opposite number, Ballet of the *Duke*. Accordingly a boat left the *Duke* with Ballet, and Page was ordered to get into it and be brought to his new ship. Page expostulated violently and refused to move, becoming so insubordinate that Cooke, the second captain, struck him. The mate hit back, and there was an undignified scuffle before he was forced into the boat and brought aboard the *Duke*.

Here neither reason nor authority could subdue him. At the first opportunity he jumped into the sea and attempted to swim back to his old ship. The boat put off once more, caught him, and brought him back; he was lashed to the main gears, whipped, and confined in irons for a week.

With a view to tightening up discipline, the officers instituted a search, and two men were punished for concealing a perruque, a pair of stockings, and two shirts, which they had taken from the Spanish barque.

II

It had already become clear that the arrangements for dividing the spoils, made by the owners in Bristol, were not acceptable to the men. Now, with opportunities for attack coming nearer every day and distance from the owners increasing, both officers and men were ready to modify the instructions and to seek an arrangement satisfactory to all. Some such arrangement was essential; the men's willingness to fight depended on it. They insisted that no privateer's crew was ever deprived of its right to plunder. The Council conceded this point, but reserved the right to decide what was plunder and what was not.

After long deliberation, the Council laid down that plunder, once it was so designated, should be distributed equally between the companies of the two ships, according to the scale of shares laid down for every man. The officers were to assess the value, and this was to be divided proportionately, after five per cent had been set aside for the two captains, Woodes Rogers and Courtney.

Woodes Rogers demurred to this, ungraciously recording it in his log as "much less than our due"; but the Council were too intent on their own interests to allow the captains any further privilege.

From any prize except those taken by boarding, when it would be disastrous to risk the men's attention being distracted to plunder, each sailor and landsman could keep what he took, up to the value of ten pounds. Every officer below the rank of carpenter was allowed twenty pounds; carpenter, gunners, boatswain and mate forty pounds; lieutenant and master eighty; and captains a hundred. All plunder had to be declared and valued, and punishments were decided for concealing "anything in excess of one piece-of-eight" while the assessment was being made. Evidently the Council, knowing their men, looked on total honesty as impracticable.

Additional fines and penalties were laid down to ensure that the profits should go only to those who fairly shared in the dangers. Drunkenness, desertion, disobedience, or any tendency to lurk in hiding at the time of action, carried each its appropriate penalty.

In addition to all this, the owners had promised a gratuity of a hundred pounds "to such as should signalise themselves", and there was a further reward of twenty pieces-of-eight for the man who sighted a prize of more than fifty tons' burden.

It is a pity that we have no records of the actual debate in which these variations of the owners' instructions were agreed. It would be interesting to know what Dover had to say, in his capacity as part owner; but there is no mention of his name during the negotiations. However, he bobs up immediately afterwards.

The crews were still disaffected. On the 16th of November, Cooke records, after his note on the weather "Wind variable, and much Rain at half an Hour past Twelve . . ."

One of our Men going from the ship without Leave, giving the first Lieutenant foul language, and threatening he would soon be reveng'd, was put in Irons, and his Mess-mates and Consorts desiring he might be re-leas'd, or they put in with him, seven voluntarily went into Irons.

On the 17th the two ships sighted a group of islands off the Brazilian coast, and, probably to divert the crew from their grievances, Dover put off in a pinnace to visit the nearest. On the principle, apparently, that a tortoise was much like a turtle, he brought back to the *Duke* a fine specimen, which, says Woodes Rogers, "our people eat": adding as an epitaph on the experiment, "The tortoises on this coast have a very strong taste."

Three days later the two ships approached the island of Grande, and Dover once more went ashore with two landing parties to discover whether any enemy ships were sheltering in the island's many bays. A small Portuguese vessel gave them news of a Frenchman who not long before had robbed them of their few possessions. A number of recently made graves were likewise explained as belonging to two much larger French ships, which had watered at the island nine months earlier on their way home from the South Seas, and had buried some half of their men. However, Dover could discover no present signs of any epidemic, and so a further landing party brought the empty water casks ashore, and the carpenter, helped by a friendly Portuguese, went in search of wood suitable for repairs.

A second Portuguese ship put in next day, and was found to be laden with negroes on the way to the gold mines. Pricking up their ears, Dover and his lieutenant asked the Portuguese captain where the mines were, only to find themselves confronted with a linguistic difficulty. Either the captain did not understand, or he was not going to say. The best information they could get was that the mine was several days' journey up in the country. To show that there was no ill-feeling, however, he made the Englishmen a present of some excellent sugar and a pot of sweetmeats. Disgruntled at their lack of information, they made him only a trifling return, and reluctantly turned their attention to re-stocking the ships, bartering oddments with the natives, and exploring their unfamiliar surroundings.

Setting off one morning "to take their pleasure", Dover and Vanbrugh succeeded in killing

. . . a monstrous creature . . . having quills or prickles like a hedgehog, with fur between them, and the head and tail resembled those of a monkey. It stunk intolerably, which the Portuguese told us was only the skin; that the meat of it is very delicious, and they often killed them for the table.

The stink was too much for them, however: they did not test the information.

To the voyagers, the island seemed a small paradise. Thickly wooded, with trees coming down to the water's edge, it had abundance of fresh water, with oranges and lemons and guavas growing wild in the woods, and affording endless sustenance to the monkeys which thronged them. In the small town rum and sugar and tobacco were to be had, but all three were expensive, and the tobacco was too strong even for the mariners. They were able to buy poultry and a pig or two, the latter rare and costly. Beef and mutton were cheap, but there was not much of either. However, there was abundance of Indian corn, bananas, plantains, and pineapples.

Two of the crew, allured by these attractions, deserted to the woods, but were so terrified by the monkeys and baboons that they ran down to the shore, waded out into the water, and shouted to the ship until they were fetched aboard.

Before this happened, however, an incident had taken place which was to have many repercussions. At four o'clock in the morning a canoe was sighted from the quarter-deck and hailed by the watch. It made no reply, and Woodes Rogers suspected that it contained the two deserters, or else was going to the island to take them off. He therefore ordered two boats to go in pursuit. Vanbrugh the agent, who

was in the first boat, acting entirely on suspicion, and without any
authority from the captain, ordered the men to open fire on the canoe.
They discharged several rounds, and hit one of the Indians who was
paddling.

When they reached the shore, Vanbrugh discovered that the canoe
was owned and was being steered by a friar, who had a quantity of
gold from the mines on board, and was using the island as a hiding
place.

The friar ran away into the woods as soon as the canoe's prow
touched the beach, but a Portuguese sailor induced him to come out
of hiding, and he and the wounded Indian were taken aboard the
Duke. The Indian's wounds were dressed, but he died within the hour.
Woodes Rogers did his utmost to pacify the friar, and accompanied
him to the shore to recover the gold, valued at two hundred pounds,
which he said had been in the canoe. Unfortunately, it had disappeared.
Woodes Rogers reports the friar as "uneasy" rather than incensed, but
he threatened none the less to go to law, in Portugal or in England,
and seek redress for the loss of his money and the death of his slave.

This incident was unfortunate in more ways than one. Even if
the lawsuit did not materialize, the unprovoked attack and the death
of the Indian had violently prejudiced the inhabitants against the
Englishmen. The Council was summoned, and a memorandum drawn
up which laid the blame for the whole incident squarely upon
Vanbrugh. This second indiscretion of the agent was too much for
Woodes Rogers, who refused to have him any longer on board the
Duke. He was therefore exchanged to the *Duchess*, where Courtney
determined to give him no further chance of causing trouble.

Fortunately, the odium arising from this incident was partly
offset by a happy occasion on the following day, when both ships'
companies were invited by the town authorities to join in celebrating
the feast of the Conception of the Blessed Virgin. There was an immense
procession, preceded by images, flowers, incense, forty priests and
friars, and the two captains, Woodes Rogers and Courtney, each
carrying a long wax candle. The Englishmen provided their own
musicians, two trumpets and a haut-boy, and the company marched
with magnificent solemnity to the unorthodox strains of "Hey boys, up
we go".

All were splendidly entertained, when the ceremonies were over,
by the Father of the convent, but Dover sardonically observed the lack
of plate and decided, with his brother officers, that the hosts were not
entirely easy in their minds about their guests' intentions.

All doubts were dispelled, however, when in return the *Duke* magnificently entertained the gentlemen of the town. Cordiality increased as the hour grew late.

They were very merry, and in their cups proposed the Pope's health to us; but we were quits with them by toasting that of the Archbishop of Canterbury.

Letters were entrusted to them, and presents of butter and cheese given as parting gifts. When the time came for going ashore, difficulties were experienced which Woodes Rogers, in his journal, tactfully attributes to the weather. When next morning the visitors were able to leave, they were sped on their way with cheers instead of the customary salute of guns, "because we were not overstocked with powder".

III

Before they left Grande, the voyagers had learned a good deal about life on the mainland of Brazil, and particularly in Buenos Aires. Agriculturally, the land seemed a paradise. There were woods of peach, of almond and fig trees, and pastures so "fat and large" as to feed cattle by the thousand. The Englishmen heard with amusement a good deal of anti-clerical gossip, chiefly to the effect that the missionaries lived so luxuriously in the town that the natives from the village were not allowed in, lest they be disillusioned about their spiritual pastors and masters. The pretext for keeping them out was that the town was a wicked place, and would corrupt them.

Early in December the two ships left Grande and pushed their way southwards into windy weather. The rough seas which they now struggled across produced new creatures. Great grampuses disported themselves, and porpoises "of an uncommon sort" leaped high from the water, their white bellies gleaming as they fell.

Soon the wind stiffened; storms and driving gales attacked the ships and pounded them with ceaseless heavy waves. On December 18th one of the *Duchess's* men fell from the mizzen top to the quarter-deck and broke his skull. Courtney sent to the *Duke* for a surgeon, and Woodes Rogers himself came with two, but they pronounced him "irrecoverable". He died and was buried the following day.

The wind dropped, and the weather was once more fine and warm. Christmas Day was spent in passing the Falkland Islands, with no

G

better diversion than watching the grampuses and the porpoises. Then in the late afternoon, a sail was sighted. Both frigates chased her til nightfall, and next morning, when the haze cleared, she was stil within view. There was however hardly any breeze to help either hei or her pursuers. The nearest they came to her was four miles, and sh was presently lost, to the discomfiture of both men and officers. The had now been at sea for four months, and had met no ship of any rea value.

New Year's Day, however, brightened the monotony of the voyage A large tub of punch was served hot on the quarter-deck, the ratio being a pint to each man. Toasts were drunk to the owners, to friends to a happy New Year, to a prosperous voyage and a safe return, anc each ship wound up by giving her consort three rousing cheers.

Soon after the New Year the ships rounded the Cape and enterec upon what was to be the most profitable and the most dangerous par of their voyage.

ELEVEN

NOW, with a suddenness which dismayed all but the few who had experienced it before, climate and weather changed. Gone were the warm tropical days, the early morning calms and the light breezes. No longer was the night sea streaked and jewelled with phosphorescence, so brilliant that a panic-stricken sailor on his watch had fetched up Woodes Rogers to the moonlit deck to look at it. Gone even was the "cold airy weather" which for a day or two had heralded the change. In place of it came stormy winds that sharpened to gale force, pounding and battering the ships with ceaseless violent waves. Now, too late, the crew regretted the warm clothing they had bartered to the natives.

The problem was to keep the men in health. The Captains had foreseen the change, and had done their best to provide for it. Six tailors had been busy making up the coarse woollen cloth that had been laid in against such an emergency, and the officers handed over all that they could spare from their own stores; but little enough could be done against the seas which swept across the decks. The *Duchess* was in the worse case. She shipped water dangerously, and her crew, drenched and shivering, were plunged in an extreme of misery.

Cooke, aboard the *Duchess*, gives a vivid account of their plight:

. . . our Waste was fill'd with Water and we expecting the ship would sink every Moment got down our Fore-yard as well as we could and loosed the Sprit-sail . . . and at Nine shipp'd a Sea at the Poop, as we were in the Cabbin going to eat; it beat in all the Cabbin Windows and Bulk-Head, and hove the first Lieutenant half way between the Decks, with several Muskets and Pistols that hung there, darting a Sword that was against the Bulk-Head of the Cabbin, through my Man's Hammock and Rug, which hung against the Bulk-Head of the Steeridge, and had not the Bulk-Head of the great Cabbin given way, all we who were there must inevitably have been drown'd, before the Water should have been vented. Our Yaul was stow'd on the Deck, and it was a Wonder that many were not kill'd with the Shutters, the Bulk-Head, and the Arms, which were drove with a prodigious Force; but God in his Mercy deliver'd us from this and many other Dangers.

Only one Man or two were hurt, and some bruis'd, but not one Rag of dr
Cloaths left us, our Chests, Hammocks and Bedding being all soak'd i
Water. . . .

Then, mercifully, came a lull. The two ships, which had bee
driven some distance apart, were able to come close and exchang
stories of the damage they had suffered. Woodes Rogers and Dampie
went aboard the *Duchess*, and "found 'em in a very orderly pickle, wit
all their clothes drying, the ship and rigging covered with 'em from th
deck to the Main-Top".

There were, however, long-term results. Damp had penetrate
to every part of the ship, and the *Duke* was not much better. This, wit
the lack of fresh meat and the long weeks at sea, at last took toll of th
men. For the first time since they left England the crews began to suffe
from weakness, colds, and scurvy, and to endure the miseries which s
commonly attended long sea voyages.

The first casualty was a landsman named John Veal. He fell i
from an unspecified disease, which caused his legs to swell, and after
fortnight's sickness died and was dropped overboard with the ceremon
and compunction due to the expedition's first loss since it left England
Veal was followed by George Cross, smith and armourer's mate,
victim to scurvy. By January 25th it was clear that most of the me
were sorely in need of a harbour, particularly those aboard the *Duchess*
Woodes Rogers became very apprehensive about them, the more so a
several of his own men were ailing, and decided that an early cal
ashore and "a small refreshment" were essential if both ships were no
to lose several men.

The ships were bound for Juan Fernandez, a small island off th
coast of Chile, but the difficulties of navigation made Woodes Roger
very doubtful whether they would find it. The officers laid their chart
side by side on the cabin table, and rubbed their heads in perplexity
since each one differed from the others.

One man, however, admitted no doubt. The irrepressible Dampie
had visited Juan Fernandez several times, and had a special reason fo
wanting to land on it again. On his first visit, twenty-eight year
earlier, the crew with whom he was sailing had been obliged to leave
man behind. A Mosbito Indian, he had gone ashore to hunt, an
remained so long that the ship sailed, leaving him alone on the unin
habited island far out of the normal path of shipping.

Three years later, in 1684, Dampier, once more cruising down th
coast, remembered the Indian and sent a man of his own race ashore tc

ook for him. The castaway, who had been watching from the shelter
•f some trees, came running out to meet his countryman, and the two
;reeted each other, first by prostrating themselves on the ground, then
;etting up and embracing.

Now, on the 21st of January 1709, when by a mixture of good
uck and good management Dampier managed to locate the island for
iis commander, he was no longer thinking of the Indian. He had been
o the island again in the interval, and another memory was vivid in
iis mind. Even so, he was in no great hurry to go ashore. A good deal
iad been happening in this part of the world, and the seas were not so
:mpty as when he sailed them first. There was always the chance
iowadays of finding Spaniards or Frenchmen, and both he and
Voodes Rogers eyed the coastline with caution. Dover, on the other
iand, would listen to no warnings. Maybe his responsibility to his
ellow owners was weighing on him. More probably, as a medical man,
ie was urged by the condition of the crews. At all events, he insisted on
aking a pinnace and going ashore to reconnoitre.

The crew of the *Duchess* watched him go with the ghoulish interest
:voked by those who insist on doing something dangerous for which
he onlookers disclaim responsibility. Woodes Rogers looked on sourly.
Ie was much annoyed by the obstinacy of his second captain. They
vere four miles from shore, and the expedition seemed to him un-
varrantable and idiotic.

As soon as the pinnace had gone, he went on board the *Duchess*,
vhere surprise was expressed at the boat going ashore when the ships
vere so far from land. Woodes Rogers called his brother officers to
vitness that the expedition was made against his will, and that he
mly consented to let the pinnace go in order to oblige Captain
Dover.

To make matters worse, darkness was coming on fast. When the
iinnace was within a league of shore, the watchers' apprehensions
vere quickened: a light appeared to be burning on the island. Peering
hrough the dusk, the crews thought they saw the pinnace turn back
owards the ship, and at once put out lights to guide the rowers; but it
vas soon too dark to be sure what was what. An excited discussion
iroke out, some of the watchers maintaining that what they were
ooking at was only a light in their own boat. Full darkness however
howed it to be too large. A second light appeared, and the officers
:oncluded that French ships were at anchor off the island.

Then the wind rose, and the two frigates drew some distance
ipart. The *Duchess* remained the closer inshore, firing guns from time

to time to show her position. Just as all were giving up hope, at two in the morning the pinnace came alongside, with her crew unharmed. They had seen the lights on the shore, but no sign of an enemy, Spanish or French.

When daylight came, the two ships tacked cautiously along the coast but could see no sign of anything suspicious. Reluctant to give up their theory, they concluded that whatever ship or ships had been there had taken fright, and made off under cover of darkness. Accordingly at midday they sent a small boat ashore with Dover, Mr. Fry and six men, fully armed. The party was seen to land but did not return. Fearing that the enemy had left a garrison on shore and that the eight men had been seized, Woodes Rogers sent the pinnace with a strong reinforcement.

In next to no time it came back, proclaiming that all were safe, and bringing a load of crawfish and, origin of the mysterious lights, "a man clothed in goatskins, who looked wilder than the first owners of them". This strange figure gave his name as Alexander Selkirk, Master of the *Cinque Ports*, and claimed that, four years and four months earlier, he had been left by the captain of his ship, to live as best he might upon the unknown island.

How, asked his hosts, could such a thing come about? Was he not left by accident, like the Indian of whom Dampier had told them? Not at all, the uncouth stranger replied. (His speech was slow and uncertain, as if he had lost the way of expressing himself.) He had had a disagreement with the captain, and the ship was so leaky that he felt he would be happier ashore. Then, when the sight of her getting ready to leave made him change his mind and wish to come on board again, the captain refused, and sailed without him.

Woodes Rogers, Dover and Courtney looked at each other, wondering whether to believe this story. Suddenly it received a dramatic confirmation.

"It is true," Dampier told them quietly. "I know this man. I was there when it happened."

Pressed for details, he said that he himself had been captain of the *St. George*, accompanying the *Cinque Ports* on her voyage. Over the actions of his brother captain he had no control, and indeed all supposed that, after his "irreconcilable difference" with Captain Stradling, Selkirk had preferred to be left ashore. Anyway, left ashore he was, on this very island, four years and four months earlier. What was more, he had been the best man aboard his ship.

On hearing this Woodes Rogers at once made Selkirk mate on

board the *Duke*. From the several accounts by the officers of the two frigates the story of his sojourn on the island emerges. An account, which purports to be Selkirk's own, says that on the previous night he saw the two ships, judged that they were English, and lit a fire to attract their attention. During his stay on the island, several ships had passed by, but only two had anchored there. Had these been French, he would have given himself up to them, but he believed them to be Spanish, and, fearing that the Spaniards would enslave or murder him, he fled into the woods. The Spaniards saw and pursued, firing shots at him, but he escaped by climbing to the top of a tree.

When he was first left alone on the island, he was permitted to take from the ship clothes and bedding, "with a firelock, some powder, bullets, and tobacco, a hatchet, a knife, a kettle, a Bible, some practical pieces and his mathematical instruments and books". With the help of these possessions he was able to provide for himself and keep his mind occupied: but for the first eight months the loneliness, and the fear of being alone in a strange place, almost overwhelmed him.

"He built two huts with pimento trees, covered them with long grass, and lined them with the skins of goats, which he killed with his gun as he wanted, so long as his powder lasted, which was but a pound, and that being near spent, he got fire by rubbing two sticks of pimento wood together upon his knee. In the lesser hut, at some distance from the other, he dressed his victuals, and in the larger he slept and employed himself in reading, singing psalms and praying: so he said that he was a better Christian while in this solitude or than he was afraid he should ever be again."

At first he ate only from extreme hunger, since loneliness and the lack of bread and salt made food unappetizing to him. Pimento wood provided fuel for his fire, "refreshed him with its fragrant smell", and, as it burnt very clearly, he could see by its light at night. He slept only when his eyes were too heavy for further watching.

He caught large crawfish, which he boiled or broiled, but found that the lack of salt made any other fish impossible to eat. His meat came from the island's many goats, with whose flesh he also made excellent broth. During his stay he killed five hundred of these animals, and caught as many more, which he released after marking them on the ear. At first he used his gun for hunting, but he soon exhausted his supply of powder, and was obliged to catch the goats by running after them, an exercise which greatly improved his health and agility.

On one occasion his enthusiasm for the chase almost cost him his life. He captured his quarry "on the brink of a precipice of which he

was not aware, the bushes having hid it from him; so that he fell with
the goat down the precipice a great height". When he recovered
consciousness, the goat was dead beneath him, and he was unable to
move for twenty-four hours. Then he crawled painfully the mile to his
hut, and lay there for ten days.

After some time he became used to the unseasoned food, and
discovered that he could add variety to his meals by using turnips
which Captain Dampier's men had sowed, cabbage from the cabbage
trees, and pimentos. "He found there also a black pepper called
Malagita, which was very good to expel wind, and against griping of
the guts."

When his constant running wore out his shoes, he had no choice but
to run without them. His feet became so hard that this ceased to trouble
him: but, when he was rescued, his feet swelled every time he put on a
pair of shoes.

He found some alleviation for his loneliness in the company of
many cats. He tamed these animals to keep away the rats which otherwise gnawed his feet and clothes as he slept. Both cats and rats had
come to the island from ships which had anchored there, and they had
bred in vast numbers. He also tamed a number of kids. To entertain
himself, he sang and danced with his cats—a curious spectacle, if
anyone had been there to see it.

Thus, by degrees, he became accustomed to his solitude, and was
able to adapt himself completely to his strange circumstances, even
contriving to make his own implements, and to renew the clothes
which had worn out.

"When his clothes wore out he made himself a coat and cap of
goats-skins, which he stitched together with little thongs of the same,
which he cut with a knife. He had no other needle but a nail, and when
his knife was worn to the back, he made others as well as he could, of
some iron hoops that were left ashore, which he beat thin and ground
upon stones. Having some linen cloth by him, he sewed himself shirts
with a nail and stitched them with the worsted of his old stockings,
which he pulled out on purpose."

The four solitary years had had their effect on him in more than
outward appearance: "At his first coming aboard, he had so much
forgotten his language for want of use, that we could scarce understand
him, for he seemed to speak his words by halves," wrote his rescuers.
When he was offered a dram, "He would not touch it, having drank
nothing but water since his being there; and it was some time before he
could relish our victuals."

Sir Richard Steele, "who had the pleasure frequently to converse with the man soon after his arrival in England", was curious about the effect of such isolation on his mind, and gives more account of his mental suffering than did the sailors. He found that while Selkirk's physical needs were easily satisfied, he suffered so intensely from lack of human companionship that he was "scarce able to refrain from doing himself violence". He was only able to overcome this state of mind by frequently reading his Bible, and applying himself assiduously to the study of navigation.

He struggled for months to overcome his loneliness, and, when the battle was over, he was amply rewarded by the pleasure which he was now able to find in the life he led. "He now taking delight in everything, made the hut in which he lay, by ornaments which he cut down from a spacious wood on the side of which it was situated, the most delicious bower, fanned with delicious breezes and gentle aspirations of wind, that made his repose after the chase equal to the most sensual of pleasures."

So that he might not lose the power of speech, he performed his devotions aloud, regularly, and in places set aside for the purpose.

Incidentally, Selkirk's return to civilization was not the altogether happy release it was everywhere supposed to be. When he returned to England, he soon found himself regretfully missing the tranquillity in which he had lived for so long.

"When I first saw him," wrote Steele, "I could discern that he had been much separated from company, from his aspect and gesture; there was a strong but cheerful seriousness in his look, and a certain disregard to the ordinary things about him, as if he had been sunk in thought. . . . He most frequently bewailed his return to the world, which could not, he said, with all its engagements, restore him to the tranquillity of his solitude. . . . To use his own expression, 'I am now worth £800, but shall never be so happy as when I was not worth a farthing.'"

II

For the privateers the island of Juan Fernandez seemed the answer to all their problems. Approximately triangular in shape, it was "about twelve leagues round", and a small island, almost a mile long, lay near it. The two frigates anchored in the shelter of the wooded shore, and the crew, who had not set foot on land for nearly two months, were set to build tents, to collect fire-wood, and to go in search of food and fresh water.

The warm, summer days, the cool breezes, the fish caught in the rock pools and cooked over wood fires, the broth of turnip tops and goats'-flesh, the abundant herbs and water-cress, were a delightful cure for the ravages of the voyage. The sick men were taken ashore, and all but two of the twenty-one recovered, nourished on Alexander Selkirk's "excellent broth", and doctored with herbs by the surgeons. Seals were caught and eaten by the men, who said that they preferred them to the ship's victuals, and that they tasted as good as English lamb. Woodes Rogers, whose taste made no concession to circumstances, declined the dish, and would allow no comparison whatever to lamb.

Sea-lions interested many of the officers, who had not seen them before. Woodes Rogers wrote of them that in the shape of their body they differed very little from seals, but that their skins were quite unlike, their heads much bigger in proportion, their mouths very large, and their eyes "monstrous big". The whole appearance of their face reminded him of that of a lion, and especially their whiskers, the hair of which was stiff enough to make toothpicks.

Cooke adds to the picture:

"In every Bay there are such Multitudes of great Sea-Lions, and Seals of several Sorts, all with excellent Furs, that we could scarce walk along the Shore for them, as they lay about in Flocks, like Sheep, the young ones bleating like lambs. Some of the Sea-Lions are as big as our English Oxen, and roar like Lions . . . we were forced to drive them away before we could land, being so numerous, that it is scarce credible to those who have not seen them; and they make a most prodigious Noise."

Their main use to the crews, however, was to furnish oil for frying. There were plenty of goats on the island. The first of them had been put ashore by the Spaniard Juan Fernandez, who settled there with a handful of his country folk until Chile submitted to Spanish rule; and they had bred abundantly. These animals were a source of constant entertainment to the crew, who made many unsuccessful efforts to catch them. Their failure was more than made up for by the fun of watching Alexander Selkirk, who leapt over the rocks with astonishing agility in pursuit. His speed as he threaded his way through the trees, or galloped up the rocky hills, was quite beyond the voyagers, even though the nimblest amongst them were chosen to help him. He even out-distanced a bulldog belonging to one of the crew, "catched the goats", and brought them triumphantly on his back.

Woodes Rogers, in the meantime, was enjoying himself more peacefully:

'Tis very pleasant ashore among the green pimento trees, which cast a refreshing smell. Our house was made by putting up a sail round four of 'em and covering it atop with another sail; so that Captain Dover and I both thought it a very agreeable seat, the weather being neither too hot nor too cold.

The island and its pleasures were inducing a spirit of tolerant good-humour in all the officers. This was the one idyllic interlude in the voyage. In the general expansiveness even Mr. Vanbrugh was forgiven, and allowed to return to the *Duke* in place of Mr. Bath. Woodes Rogers noted the transfer, charitably abating his misgivings. "I hope for the best," he wrote.

By February 14th the work of the smiths, the coopers, and the sail-makers had been completed, the ships had been re-victualled, and all arrangements for sailing made. The officers of the *Duke* dined on board the *Duchess*, and the cruise began once more in a spirit of happiness and goodwill.

"God be thanked we have good concord between each ship's company."

TWELVE

FOR a month the two ships cruised in fine pleasant weather within sight of the coast of Chile. The days were uneventful, and the crew very much the better for their spell on shore. The only casualty during these weeks was a boy who fell out of the *Duchess's* mizzen-top, and broke his leg, but was pronounced "in a fair way to recover". On March 16th they captured a small Spanish Indian trader, put in at Lobos, and fitted her up as a small privateer, rechristened *The Beginning*. She was given to Captain Cooke as his command. At the same time, the Council made arrangements that the three ships should now cruise independently, using Lobos as a base. In case they were accidentally separated, either by constraint in battle, or choice in pursuing a possible prize, they were to leave a glass bottle buried near "a remarkable great stone", with letters describing their plans and naming a meeting place when individual operations were over.

Before setting off on any such jaunt, however, Woodes Rogers was anxious about the condition of the *Duke*. Delayed for one day by the sudden death of a Spaniard named Sylvester Ramos, and the cere-monial of burying him, he beached the *Duke* and scrubbed her bottom thoroughly, clearing away barnacles the size of mussels. "The ship grows foul very fast in these waters," he observed. For the rest there was abundance of good fishing, and the pursuit of seals, of which they found plenty, though not so many as at Juan Fernandez. This game had its dangers, however. One of the largest seals attacked a stout Dutchman, biting him to the bone in several places, and would have dragged him into the water if his comrades had not managed to rescue him. This Dutchman recovered, but one of his countrymen on the *Duchess*, a case of scurvy who had been landed on the island, died there and was buried.

The seals offered another kind of danger. The crews killed several of them and ate their livers. After the first meal, a Spaniard suddenly died, and Woodes Rogers forbade the others to touch them. The prisoners backed up this decision by saying that the old seals were "very unwholesome". They certainly smelt bad, and the steady breeze that blew from the shore brought the smell to the ships. Everyone complained of it, and Woodes Rogers averred that it gave him a violent headache.

Seals were not the only island creatures that smelt bad. There were a great many birds variously described by the voyagers as vultures and carrion crows. Vultures was probably nearer the mark, since Woodes Rogers says the birds looked very like turkeys.

. . . One of our officers at landing blessed himself at the sight, and hoped to fare deliciously . . . He was so eager that he could not stay till the boat put him ashore, but leaped into the water with his gun, and getting near enough to a parcel, let fly at 'em, but when he came to take up his game it stank insufferably and made us merry at his mistake.

Happily, however, there was plenty of more wholesome game: penguins, pelicans, "boobys", gulls, and small birds rather like teal, which nestled in hollowed-out holes on the sand and so were easy to capture. The men caught them in great numbers, skinned them, and declared that they were delicious.

On the afternoon of April 2nd, the crew were suddenly astonished to find that the water as far as they could see looked red as blood. Those who were scientifically curious investigated, and found that the phenomenon was due to the spawn of fish.

Then at last came action. Some Spanish Indians told Woodes Rogers that the *Cinque Ports*, the ship on which Alexander Selkirk had been sailing when he was marooned, had foundered on their coast. Only six or seven men had struggled to the shore, and these had been imprisoned at Lima ever since. Selkirk himself was made Master of the next prize, which was renamed *The Increase*, and Mr. Fry was given command of yet another. The little fleet was on the point of splitting up when news came that two rich ships were expected at Payta, and the Council decided to stay off Lobos, in the hope of intercepting them. One was believed to be carrying the widow of the late Viceroy of Peru to Acapulca, and the other was bringing a bishop from Panama.

On April 15th they sighted the latter, a French ship, and decided gleefully that she was carrying the bishop, because of the white satin flag with a fringe which she hoisted. The attack was successful, they captured the ship, but found to their chagrin that the bishop and all his plate had been disposed of ten days earlier.

The other ship brought them even less success; for when the attacking party approached her in two pinnaces, they were themselves fired on before they could manœuvre into a good position, and were forced to withdraw with a loss of two men and another badly wounded. One of these deaths caused the whole company real grief. It was John Rogers, the captain's brother.

About twelve we read the Prayers for the Dead, and threw my dear brother overboard, with one of our sailors . . . We hoisted our colours but half mast up. We began first, and the rest followed, firing each some volleys of small arms. Our officers expressed a great concern for the loss of my brother, he being a very hopeful, active young man, a little above twenty years of age.

II

Strengthened by the recent additions to their little fleet, the privateers now made plans for an attack on the mainland. After some argument they chose for their landing place the small Spanish town of Guaiaquil. The officers felt none too sure of the fighting capacities of the men under their command, who, although by now they had been knocked into a reasonable likeness to sailors, had met no real test against organized resistance. Picking their men carefully, they formed three landing parties under the leadership of Captain Dover, Captain Woodes Rogers, and Captain Courtney. Detailed plans for attack were drawn up, and, to prevent the men from straggling when they landed, each was given a ticket, so that he should remember what company he belonged to.

Plunder was clearly defined. It was to include bedding, clothes "without stripping", necessaries, gold rings, buckles, buttons, liquors, provisions, all arms and ammunition, crucifixes and watches made of silver and gold, and other "moveables" found in the possession of prisoners. It did not include money, precious stones, or ear rings. The rules on the declaration and sharing of plunder were once more proclaimed. Finally:

. . . to prevent all manner of pernicious and mischievous ill-conduct that may accrue by disorders ashore, we pressingly remind you, that any officer or other that shall be so brutish as to be drunk ashore in an enemy's country, shall not only be severely punished, but lose all share of whatsoever is taken in this expedition.

On the 17th of April the preparations were completed. The frigates and the prizes anchored thirty-six leagues off shore, and the three boats approached Guaiaquil in the darkness. The precedence of Dover's name was not accidental. Woodes Rogers and Courtney being, as they put it, "willing to compliment him", agreed that he should be in command of the landing. This operation he managed without harm, although the wind freshened and the sea became rather rougher than was comfortable for boats "deep laden and crammed with men". It also made the rowing difficult, "but in regard we are about a charming undertaking, we think no fatigue too hard". A couple of days after landing they attacked and captured an outpost.

Unfortunately some of the enemy escaped, and a Spanish paper found on a prisoner contained a warning to all ships that the redoubtable Captain Dampier was cruising the coast, plus instructions to keep severe watch and to remove all valuables and provisions to a place of safety. There was thus little hope of finding the Spaniards unprepared.

It was impossible to attack the town until nightfall, and a party spent a most uncomfortable day lurking in the heat of the mangrove swamps, tormented by mosquitos. All tempers suffered, particularly those of the officers. When at last darkness came, and they were able to emerge from their malodorous retreat, get into their boats, and row stealthily along the river, they saw to their dismay that a fire was burning on a hill, and there were lights everywhere in the town. It was obvious that the alarm had been given, and that the enemy were on the *qui vive*.

Woodes Rogers ordered the men to stop rowing, and for a while they drifted, carried by the tide. Suddenly the voice of a Spaniard rang out from the shore, telling his companions that the outpost had been taken, and that the enemy were coming up the river. Then came a volley of small arms, directed at no one in particular, and bells began to ring. Their boats close together, the three captains debated for over an hour whether or not to land. Woodes Rogers urged that they should attack immediately while the town was in consternation. Dover said that even the buccaneers never ventured to take a large place once it had been given the alarm. While they were still arguing, the tide turned, making any attack impossible until next morning.

Cooke has an amusing note on this episode. While the officers were disputing, their voices rose to such a pitch as to be heard by the Spaniards on shore. Not understanding what was said, they sent for an interpreter; but by the time he reached them, the argument was over.

The boats rowed further down the river, where they spent the night, and were joined by reinforcements from the *Duke* and *Duchess*. Dover now called for a discussion between all the officers. In order to conceal their disagreement from the men, they held it in a boat well astern of the others. It at once appeared that what Dover wanted was a confirmation of his own point of view. He took charge of the discussion immediately, insisting on the difficulties of the attack and the probability of casualties which, without any certain prospect of compensating gain, might wreck the success of the whole expedition. The town was large, he told them, and the mulattoes would all be armed. Because of all this, and with other reasons "not fit to recite here", he proposed that they should give up all idea of the attack, and try instead to trade the goods which were on board the prizes.

Woodes Rogers brushed all this aside. A sudden attack, made without delay, offered every prospect of success. Whether from a sense of solidarity against the landsman, or because his arguments convinced them, the majority of the officers took his side. Magnanimous as always, he attempted to salve Dover's wounded dignity by suggesting that he should lead the attack and give the watchword on the first night ashore.

Far from appeasing Dover, this only increased his opposition. He replied icily that he wanted no part in the attack, though he would of course obey the majority decision, but that he would hold Woodes Rogers personally answerable for any damage that might result. A proportion of the officers, if not positively opposed to the landing, showed no enthusiasm for it, so that Woodes Rogers's confidence in the success of the attack was undermined.

III

In view of these doubts, which he kept to himself, Woodes Rogers managed to arrange a parley with the Corregidor, the official in command on shore. No difficulty was put in the way, the Corregidor agreeing to come at eight o'clock "with other gentlemen" and discuss the propositions put to him by the Englishmen. The three captains prepared the best entertainment they could muster away from their ships, and had candles lit aboard the *Duke's* boat, which had brought them their reinforcements. But the Corregidor did not appear. Suspecting some form of trick, they were very wary when presently a messenger came instead, bringing presents of wine and brandy, hogs, sheep, and

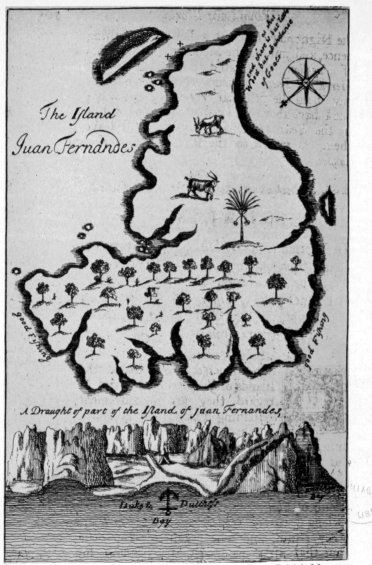

The Island
Juan Fernándes

A Draught of part of the Island of Juan Fernandes,

CAPTAIN EDWARD COOKE'S MAP
OF JUAN FERNANDEZ

CAPTAIN EDWARD COOKE'S DRAWINGS OF
SOME OF THE ANIMALS SEEN ON HIS VOYAGE

flour, and suggesting that they should meet for a conf rence on the following morning.

The conference took place, however; and the Englishmen, emboldened, offered two ships, and six smaller vessels which they had captured in the river, in exchange for fifty thousand pieces of eight and a promise that the Spaniards should buy from them the negroes and the goods which they had found aboard their prizes.

After some chaffering, the Corregidor compromised at forty thousand pieces of eight, and the English, who had purposely pitched their demands high, were satisfied with the bargain. Getting their money was quite another matter. Twice the suave Spanish officer put them off with excuses, and, suspecting that he was playing for time, they issued an ultimatum and decided to attack. Leaving only a few on the reinforcement boats to cover their landing, three boatloads of men went ashore, taking with them two guns on their field carriages.

They found the enemy strongly posted in the houses of the main street, with a line of horse at its end, and four guns trained on them in front of a church. Undismayed by this array, the privateers landed, formed up at the water's edge, dropped each man on one knee, fired a volley, and reloaded. Then, dividing into three groups, they advanced, but almost at once broke all order and rushed on the enemy, capturing the guns and driving all before them. Somehow the officers got them under control, marched them through the town, and occupied the three churches, where they took cover and spent the night.

Dover, who in spite of his sentiments had consented to lead the attack, now found himself in an unenviable position. His church was on the outskirts of the town, too far away for him to get help from the others if he were attacked, and overhung by a wooded hill which gave ample cover to the enemy. As a precaution he set the houses nearest him on fire, but the Spaniards hid in the trees and were "continually popping at him all night". In the morning he abandoned it, as being too exposed to defend, and joined the others, to find that all systematic opposition was over, and the town was theirs.

The casualties were astonishingly few, and most of them inflicted by their own side. The Spaniards seem to have accounted only for two, whose wounds Dover did not think dangerous. A Portuguese named Martin was killed by the misbehaviour of a small mortar aboard the reinforcement boat. Acting on "a too severe order" to shoot anyone at night that did not give the password, a Frenchman whom Woodes Rogers had sent to strengthen Courtney's party shot and killed an Englishman named Hugh Tidcomb. Mr. Stratton, Courtney's first

H

lieutenant, got a bullet in the thigh from one of his own pistols hanging at his side. Another man, shot in the calf of his leg, "by his irregularity and hard drinking fell into a fever which carried him off".

The parties now began a systematic plundering of the town. It was soon apparent that the Spaniards had used the time gained by parleys and promises to remove their treasure, and a boat was sent up the river to look for it. The rest, having found enough plunder to whet their appetite, discovered by the stench in one of the churches that a number of bodies had only recently been buried there, and wanted to tear up the floor and search them. Dover at once put his foot down, because of the danger of fever, and the corpses were left alone.

The Spaniards made occasional half-hearted attempts to harass them while the plundering was going on, and there were a few petty skirmishes, but nothing of note. The weather turned savagely hot, and it was with relief that the officers saw the party return from up the river—where it had been all but lost. Woodes Rogers thereupon ordered all plunder to be carried aboard the reinforcement boats, and sent a demand for ransom to the Corregidor.

The river party had found no very substantial treasure, but their expedition had been well worth while. The houses up the river were full of women. One house in particular held more than a dozen, all of whom were declared to be young, handsome, and "genteel". The men took from them a number of gold chains and earrings, but in so courteous and well-behaved a manner that the ladies fetched out a "cask of good liquor" and "offered to dress them victuals". The extent of the men's courtesy was shown by the fact that the ladies had attempted to conceal their most valuable chains by winding them about their waists, their legs, and their thighs; but, as Woodes Rogers ingenuously explains, in those hot countries gentlewomen did not wear very much, and what they wore was thin, silk and fine linen. The Englishmen, "by pressing with their hands on the outside of the ladies' apparel", detected the chains, and through the interpreters "modestly desired the gentlewomen to take 'em off and surrender 'em".

Woodes Rogers is at pains to make this clear, not only as a proof of the sailor's modesty, but in respect to Mr. Connely and Mr. Selkirk, who were in command of the party. He thought it all the more remarkable in that they were young men, and hoped that when they returned to England, the ladies there would use them gratefully in return for their self-restraint and circumspection towards "these charming prisoners".

On April 27th, after another day of small forays in which the English took no harm, the Spaniards signed an agreement acknowledging the English masters of Guaiaquil, and undertaking to pay the ransom within six days. All fighting was now at an end, and the men, sick of being soldiers, marched back to the boats. Woodes Rogers brought up the rear, picking up pistols, cutlasses, and pole-axes, mightily relieved to get them away before their carelessness and demoralization brought the expedition to harm.

Once on board, the officers of each ship called the roll, and accounted for all their crews except one Dutchman. They waited for a while, stowing away the plunder and other gear, in hopes that he would turn up. He had disobeyed an urgent injunction: but, in the general pleasure and relief at the outcome of the attack, he seems to have been welcomed rather then reproved.

April 28th. At two yesterday afternoon our Dutchman that was missing arose out of his brandy-wine fit and came aboard; he was disturbed by the honest man of the house where he lay, who first called in his neighbours and cautiously seized his arms, then gently raised him, and when his eyes were opened, told him there was his arms again, and bid him hasten aboard to us.

Certainly the operation had been a success. The plunder amounted to twelve hundred pounds' worth of plate, and earrings, and jewels, a hundred and fifty bales of dried goods, two hundred and thirty bags of flour, beans, peas, and rice: a hundred and sixty jars of miscellaneous liqueurs: fifteen jars of oil: quantities of sugar, cocoa, indigo, and anotto: a number of weapons, and a fine collection of iron-ware, nails, cordage, pitch, tar, and other useful items for the voyage.

The whole party therefore set off in good spirits, their one regret being that they had failed to take the town by surprise. By the time they reached the frigates, however, reaction had set in. They became aware that they were tired, and grew increasingly uneasy lest the Spaniards should have sent messages for help and bring enemy ships in pursuit.

This uneasiness became so acute that Courtney urged setting sail at once. Woodes Rogers wished to give the crews a good night's rest, but both Dampier and Dover voted with Courtney and, since Woodes Rogers refused to budge, they sailed off, leaving the *Duke* and the other ships at anchor. The laugh was against them, however. A calm set in, and they made no speed, so that the others came up with them, rested, in the morning. Woodes Rogers did his utmost to convince them that they were in no danger, as any Spanish attack would have to come from Lima, and there had not been time for a message to bring ships from so far off; but by now their nerve was thoroughly shaken. Hardly waiting for the full ransom to be handed over—another indication that Woodes Rogers's reasoning was right, since the Spaniards would have made excuses for delay if they had any hope of a reserve party—they put to sea, and, leaving Guaiaquil and its dangers to the south, sailed along the coast towards Mexico and California.

THIRTEEN

TENSION between the officers was now growing acute, and the events of the next few weeks helped to increase it. So far, Dover, carefully handled by Woodes Rogers, had kept his ill-defined place and given little trouble. The lack of sympathy between him and his commander had led to nothing serious, and the experience of the sea-farers, reinforced by that of Dampier, had kept the balance. Now an emergency, dealt with in spectacular fashion by Dover, thrust him into the forefront, and encouraged a number of the officers to take his part and play him off against Woodes Rogers to their own advantage.

Certainly Dover handled the emergency with authority and success. What gave him his confidence is hard to say. The circumstances must have been new to him: Bristol can scarcely have produced the brand of fever with which he was now confronted. His own account of the matter is worth quoting, if only for the light which the first sentence throws on his character:

When I took by storm the two cities of Guaiaquil, under the line, in the South Seas, it happened that not long before the Plague had raged amongst them. For our better security, therefore, and keeping our people together, we lay in their churches: and likewise brought thither the plunder of the city. We were very much annoyed with the smell of dead bodies. These bodies could hardly be said to be buried, for the Spaniards abroad use no coffins, but throw several dead bodies one upon another, with only a draw board over them: so 'tis no wonder we received the infection.

In a very few days after we got on board, one of the Surgeons came to me to acquaint me, that several of my men were taken after a violent manner, with that languor of spirits. I immediately went among them, and to my great surprise, discerned what was the matter. In less than 48 hours we had in our ships 180 men in this condition.

I ordered the Surgeons to bleed them in both arms and to go round to them all with command to leave them bleeding till all were blooded, and then come and tie them up in their turns. Thus they lay bleeding and fainting, so long, that I could not conceive they could lose less than an hundred ounces each man.

If we had lost so great a number of our people, the poor remains must infallibly have perished. Now if we had had recourse to Alexipharmicks such as Venice Treacle, Diacodium, Mithridate and such like good-for-nothing compositions, or the most celebrated Gascoin's powder, or Bezoar, I make no question at all, considering the heat of the climate, but we had lost every man. 'Tis surprising to me that Physicians can read so many authors, and overlook the most reasonable rules of Mankind, and imbibe principles which, were it not for fear of giving offence, I should say were contrary to common-sense.

Leaving aside the aspersion on Alexipharmicks, etc., this account is confirmed by the two chroniclers. Only eleven men died. However performed, it was an astonishing feat of medicine, and it enormously raised Dover's standing with the entire expedition.

This fact emerges rather from what happened later than from any explicit comment made by either chronicler at the time.[1] Dover, in his own account, characteristically took full credit for the men's recovery. Woodes Rogers attributed the fact that the plague did not spread throughout the crews to his own preventive measure, i.e. large quantities of punch; but he permitted himself to wonder, in his journal, that the doctors should be short of medical supplies when the ordering of them had been left in their hands. Where the whole expedition was at fault, of course, was in not having a medical man with experience of the conditions which they were likely to meet. No landsman, un-prompted, would anticipate two hundred cases of the same disease.

The most serious loss was the death of Dover's own brother-in-law, Samuel Hopkins. "A very good-tempered sober man, and very well loved by the whole ship's company," he had read prayers every day to the assembled men.

The disease and its consequences made conditions hard, and demoralized the crews. Water was becoming dangerously short, what bread they had left was full of worms, and the prisoners, taking advantage of the general upset, laid a plot to murder their captors. Even Woodes Rogers was forced to admit that "everything looks dull and discouraging".

Then, just in time, the ships reached the island of Gorgona, and put in thankfully to water and careen, and to recover from their disaster. Two prizes which had been taken were ransomed, thanks to negotiations by some negro prisoners, and one of them, the *Havre de Grace*, was refitted and christened the *Marquis*. On board this ship the

[1] See Appendix D.

English found great numbers of bones in small boxes, labelled with the names of "Romish saints". She held also no less than thirty tons of medals, crosses, beads, crucifixes, and images of wood, stone, and even of wax, which were being taken from Italy to the Jesuits of Peru. Disconcerted by all this, and with some degree of unwilling respect for its purposes, the crews took samples only, to show their friends in England. The more unwieldy objects were thrown overboard. A party of prisoners allowed on shore under guard found one of the largest wooden effigies washed up on the shore. Regarding this as a happy omen, they wiped it dry, and set it up. When, not unnaturally, it kept sweating moisture, they cried out that this was a miracle, and, wiping away the moisture with pieces of cotton, treasured them as relics. Woodes Rogers shook his head in wonder, but did not interfere.

The other prize, the *Panama*, had passengers who, now that they were taken prisoner, occasioned the officers some slight embarrassment. These were a Spanish gentlewoman and her family. The eldest daughter, a very pretty girl of eighteen, was newly married and in the company of her husband. The captains assigned the great galley aboard the *Havre de Grace* to this family, and allowed no one, not even the officers, to intrude upon their company or attempt in any way to separate them. As a further safeguard, the third lieutenant of the *Duke*, by name Glendall, was put in charge of both ship and prisoners. Being over fifty,

he appeared to be the most secure guardian to females that had the least charm, though all our young men have hitherto appeared modest beyond example among privateers. Yet we thought it improper to expose them to temptation.

In spite of these precautions, the young lady's husband showed all the signs of jealousy, which Woodes Rogers laconically terms the Spaniards' epidemic disease. That he had no grounds for it the entire family confessed when finally they were put ashore. They had not expected anything like such civil treatment, they told their captors, and they did not believe that their own countrymen would have been as considerate.

While refitting, the crews cleared a place in the woods beside the shore, where they put up tents for the convalescent men, the sail-makers, smiths, and coopers. This encampment they called, with a charming touch of sentiment, Little Bristol.

II

When the expedition put to sea once more, the newly captured *Marquis* was found to be extremely awkward—"crank" is Woodes Rogers's word for it—and to sail heavily. He therefore suggested that Captain Cooke, who had been made Master, should sail her directly to India, so that she might be ransomed without further delay.

For some reason the other captains objected to this plan, and Woodes Rogers gave way to them, expressing the fear that they would all live to regret it, if only for the sake of the extra provisions which the *Marquis* would require.

It is plain to see that by now the officers were hopelessly split into two camps, and that every decision that had to be made gave them an excuse for further difference. A continual source of quarrels was the division of the plunder, which always left some members dissatisfied, on whatever basis it was arranged.

The discovery that mutiny was threatened, involving sixty of the men, had the effect of reuniting the officers, temporarily at least, in their own defence. The plot was on too big a scale to be dealt with harshly, and it was necessary to arrange negotiations between the men and the officers. Plunder was the difficulty here too. Woodes Rogers and Courtney, by voluntarily giving up their shares, set an example which put the others to shame.

Sailors usually exceed all measures when left to themselves, and account it a privilege in Privateering to do themselves justice in these occasions, though in everything else I must own, they have been more obedient than any ship's crew engaged in the like undertaking that I ever heard of.

The officers did not, in Woodes Rogers's opinion, deserve a like testimonial. They had all been at odds for some time; "almost a general misunderstanding" is his phrase for it; and their behaviour had occasionally passed all normal bounds of disagreement. The action at Guaiaquil, which had provoked so much preliminary argument, provoked even more in retrospect. Only one thing could bring the officers together, and that was dissension among the crew. They came together, reluctantly and sullenly enough, and this demonstration of discipline made Woodes Rogers record the hope of reconciliation and good harmony, so essential to the welfare of the voyage.

This hope was not fulfilled, and on August 6th the disagreement reached such a pitch that the captains drew up a memorandum to try to keep peace between the officers and make them swear to help each other in the case of an attack.

The different ways in which the two chroniclers looked at events is shown by Cooke's brief reference to what so occupied his colleague's mind:

Sunday, October 23. . . . In this Bay I lost my Stream-Anchor, the Cable being rotten, parted, as did the Buoy-Rope. Several hot Controversies happen'd, about this Time, among some of our chief Officers, which I endeavour'd to allay and moderate, but with little Success, for which I was much concern'd. . . .

For some time after this matters seem to have been fairly peaceful, and Woodes Rogers could devote himself to comment, often amusing, on the day-to-day occurrences of the voyage. When a party landed for trade with the Indians, the sailor described proudly as "our Linguist" told them that among their prisoners was a padre of whom they all thought very well, and that, if the Indians consented to trade, the padre in reward would absolve them of their sins. The Indians rose to the bait, and asked that the padre should be allowed to come on shore. In return, a party visited the ship, including a naked Indian who examined everything with the minute care of a monkey. The captain's cabin especially astonished him. He lay down and rolled his eyes at its wonders, until Woodes Rogers, fearing for his sanity, gave him a dram of brandy, a few toys, and some old bays (green cloth) with which to clothe himself. He was then sent ashore, in the hope that the welcome he had received would influence others. Brandy soon proved to be the best password, making friends even of armed and painted Indians, who promised in return anything the visitors wanted from the village.

Before setting sail again, the English set free the padre whose good offices, both secular and religious, had proved so profitable to them.

We put our young Padre ashore, and gave him as he desired the prettiest young female negro we had in the Prize, with some bays, linen and other things for his good services in helping to promote our trade for provisions here. The young Padre parted with us extremely pleased, leering under his hood upon his black female angel. We doubt he will crack a commandment with her, and wipe off the sin with the Church's Indulgence.

At the next port of call, the men brought back turtles with them. Woodes Rogers was much struck with their ugliness. With his careful eye and his cataloguing pen, he compared their shell to the top of an old hackney coach, as black as jet. The outside skin was black too, shrivelled, and very rough. The long legs and neck he records as being "about the bigness of a man's wrist", and their elephantine club feet the size of his fist. They had, he noted, five thick nails on the forefeet, but only four behind. When at first surprised, they shrank their neck, and drew their head and legs in underneath their shell. One was so big that two of the crew climbed on its back. It did not seem to feel their weight, but carried on at its slow and dignified pace without regarding them.

Possibly this was the creature which, whether as a protest or stimulated by the exercise, proceeded to lay eggs on the deck.

Woodes Rogers himself had an adventure with a large savage seal, which made three separate attacks on him, actually coming out of the water and rushing him on the sand. Armed with an iron-pointed pike-staff, Woodes Rogers repelled each attack by wounding the brute in the breast, and at last driving him back into the water, roaring, snarling, and baring his huge teeth. This ferocious animal was as big as a large bear.

Woodes Rogers was naturally observant, and his description of the various animals is graphic and accurate. He was particularly charmed by a sloth.

He moved as if he had walked by art, keeping an equal flow and pace, as if all his movements had been directed by clockwork within him.

All in all, this was a happy interlude in the voyage, with its delicious fresh food, hares, turtle doves, pigeons, and parrots. Dampier, more daring than the others, ate monkeys, saying that no delicacy he had ever eaten in London was more delicious. The men followed his example, but not the officers. They ate and ate, turtle, fresh fruit, and everything they could lay hands on, knowing all too well that soon they would be on the seas again, having to fall back on salt pork and beef, none of it now in good condition, yet valuable because there was so little left.

Once they were away from land, trouble began to arise again, both among the officers and among the men. Dover, taking a dislike to his company, desired to be transferred from the *Duke* to the *Duchess*; and Woodes Rogers, knowing his man by now, made a special minute of this in the Council's records, emphasizing that the change was made at Dover's express choice. Soon afterwards Woodes Rogers had to order two of the crew into irons; one a sailor who had threatened a cooper, and the other, "an ill abusive fellow", who had loudly wished that an enemy strong enough to take the ship would come alongside and do so.

Soon after this the expedition reached a region of which very little was known to European navigators. They were uncertain whether California, the coastline of which now lay before them, was attached to the rest of the American continent, or whether it was an island. "I have often admired," writes Woodes Rogers, "that no considerable discoveries have yet been made in south latitude from America to the East Indies." He goes on to say, of California and Mexico, that to the best of his knowledge only three or four navigators had sailed over "the South Ocean", and that, as they had all kept to much the same course, the sum total of discovery was small. He suggests that the South Sea Company or others should systematically explore these waters, in the hope of finding a better country than any yet discovered, there being a tremendous area, limited only by the ice which it seemed reasonable to him to expect to counterbalance that about the North Pole.

Still, known or unknown, the coast of California proved most pleasant, and the Indians friendly and hospitable. Showing no fear of the visitors, they came aboard, ate what was put before them, and invited the Englishmen to go ashore with them. Surf and rollers prevented a landing by boat, and the men went ashore on bark logs, each with an Indian swimming on either side to guide him. When they reached the shore, the Indians led each guest to "an old naked gentleman" kneeling on a deer skin. Greetings over, the Indians then dried their guests "without a cloth", then led them along slowly through a narrow path to their huts, where, in order to divert and welcome them, they found "a dull musician rubbing two jagged sticks across each other, and humming to it". After further ceremonial greetings, guests and hosts sat on the ground and made a hearty meal of broiled fish, after which they were escorted back in the same manner, with strains from the same musician.

Many parties of English went ashore, and were at first perplexed by the fact that all the women of the tribe appeared to be advanced in age. The explanation, when it occurred, was partly flattering to their vanity. Evidently the Indians were afraid to let them see any of the young women and girls. However, friendly relations were maintained. The Indians proved absolutely honest, making no attempt to steal the tools which the Englishmen left lying on the shore. The only things they seemed to want were the knives, and they manifestly preferred their own necklaces of pearls, berries, and shells to the coloured glass beads offered them by the sailors.

These Indians struck the English as an indolent race, content with the most primitive living and cooking arrangements, and a minimum of personal possessions. For food they ate fruits and berries and vegetables resembling peas and yams which grew naturally and did not have to be cultivated, and whatever they chanced to catch by fishing and hunting. They watched attentively while the English cut wood and filled their water casks, but none offered to lend a hand, and at no time did the English see them engaged in anything at all resembling hard labour. They were not at all interested in clothing either. One was given a shirt, but, like a monkey, he tore it to pieces. Then, not at all like a monkey, he shared out the pieces with his companions, and they wrapped up in them the seeds which they used for bread.

The inhabitants greatly interested Cooke. He confirms Woodes Rogers's observations, and adds others of his own:

Their Arms are Bows and Arrows, with which they are excellent Marksmen, and will shoot a small Bird flying. The Bows are about six Foot long, of a hard, yet pliant Wood. The Arrows of jointed Cane, with four long Feathers, about a Foot from the Notch for the String; at the other End is fix'd into the Reed a Piece of hard Wood, pointed with a hard tapering rugged Flint. The whole length of the Arrow four Foot and a half. . . . I am of Opinion, that these Wretches might be brought to some Knowledge in the Christian Religion; but the Spaniards say not; and to the Northward of this Place, the Natives are more savage, warlike, and faithless. I know not what they worship, unless it be the Sun.

. . . Having no Pots, they toast their Fish in the Sand, and eat it with Seeds; and I believe but little Flesh, and yet are lusty strong Men. Their Way of lighting a Fire, is with a Stick slit in two, laid on a Stone the flat Side upwards, one Person holding it, then another takes a strait stick, about a Foot and a half long, and puts one End of it upon that the other holds, and so work as we do Chocolate, pressing hard on it, and working it into the flat Stick, which soon takes Fire.

The women . . . let their Children suck 'till very big, and when travelling, carry them on their Backs; they sit and lie in the Sand, like Swine.

Everyone was happy during this idyllic stay, and the crew went so far as to play practical jokes upon the surgeons, painting a few men with red lead and woefully bringing them aboard for attention. From a small prize, captured off the coast, news came that Prince George of Denmark had died—"which we were not willing to believe, but drank his health at night, which can do him no hurt if he is dead".

Another prize brought the first news of a really large ship, bound for Acapulca from Manila. This ship Dampier had failed to capture five years earlier, and Cooke believed it to be the main object of the voyage. The excitement was therefore intense when, on December 21st, the man at the mast-head sighted a sail seven leagues away and the *Duke* and *Duchess* hastened to give chase. They kept it up throughout the night, and next day Woodes Rogers, in the absence of any "spiritous liquor", ordered a kettle of chocolate to be brewed for the ship's company. They then went to prayers but were interrupted in the middle by the enemy firing on them.

Cooke, unable to get clear of the island because of a contrary wind, had to sit by and watch the *Duke* and *Duchess* go into action.

The Manila ship proved to be no match for the combined attack of the two frigates, and after a short engagement the prize was taken, at small cost except for Woodes Rogers, who was so wounded in the jaw by a round of gunshot that "his teeth dropped upon the deck where he fell" and for a long time afterwards he was unable to speak without pain. But the commander was tough, and when, the next day, a still larger ship was sighted and the frigates gave chase, he defied the surgeons and for seven hours directed the battle, receiving another wound in the foot.

In this second action Dover seems to have played no very glorious part. When the ship was sighted, and the prisoners from the other prize were put into a "bark without rudder, oars, or weapons" till the battle was over, Captain Dover decided to appoint himself in charge of them, and sent back to the *Duchess* one of the lieutenants appointed to keep guard over the prisoners.

All three ships made a violent and concerted attack.

We kept raking of her fore and aft, and then war'd to get out of the way of the *Duke's* Shot, still firing, as did the other Ships. Soon after, the *Duchess* came upon her Starboard-side, and the *Duke* follow'd very close, and so near the Chase, that she threw her Stink-Pots on Board the *Duke*, that blew up several Carriages of Powder on the Quarter-Deck; the *Duchess* being a-going to lash to the Enemy, was forc'd to cast off, and get clear, for Fear of being set on Fire. The Enemy fir'd at us all three at once, but slow, seldom missing our Masts and Rigging, and sometimes hulling us.

The *Duchess* was compelled to lay by to stop her leaks, and Captain Rogers to secure his mast. But Cooke went on firing at the enemy until the *Duke* rejoined him.

We knotted some of our rigging, and stopp'd our Leaks made with Twelve pounders. Our main-Mast was disabled also, the Sails and Rigging much shatter'd; but the Enemy aiming to disable my Masts, I had the good Fortune to have only my second Mate, and some others, blown up with Powder. The Ship was once set afire by the Enemies Stink-Pots, with which I stank several Days intolerably, but we soon put it out.

Finally, hearing from prisoners of the smaller prize the strength of the great ship ("we might as well have fought a Castle of 50 guns, as this Ship which had about 40"), and finding that they could make no impression on her, they decided to abandon the chase.

Thus the richest prize they had yet seen escaped. It was, they learned afterwards, her first voyage: she had sixty guns, and was manned by a crew of four hundred and fifty pirates, all resolute to defend her to the end. This failure exacerbated the differences between the officers of the English expedition; and, when the question arose who should command the newly captured prize, the factions at once declared themselves.

Woodes Rogers, weak from his wound, was at a disadvantage. He could not attend meetings of the Council, and was dependent on news brought to his bedside. He could, however, write up his journal: and the New Year begins on a note of protest:

Captain Courtney and his officers, with those on board the *Marquis*, are too willing to compliment Captain Dover with the chief command of the Prize; which till now I thought he would not have accepted, his posts being already above a commander of any of our prizes; but I and my officers are against it because we believe Captain Fry or others are fitter persons to take charge of her, which we insisted on. . . .

Courtney and Cooke came to Woodes Rogers's cabin, and after some discussion, in which again Woodes Rogers was handicapped by the pain it cost him to speak, a paper was drawn up which satisfied him and which he was convinced would satisfy everyone else. The two officers then left him to get Dover's signature to the document. To his amazement, however, they did not return till the day after, and with a very different tale. Instead of persuading Dover to comply with the agreement, they brought an entirely new one, empowering Dover to be sole commander of the prize, with no proviso at all to restrict him from interfering with her navigation or in anything else, however specialized, that might take his fancy.

Weak but unshaken in his beliefs, Woodes Rogers refused his consent. Cooke and Courtney once more withdrew, and when, on the next day, January 3rd, he sent for Courtney to know what was going on,

They were then all aboard the *Marquis*, where I heard they had, ever since our last meeting, concerted how to frame a protest against me and my officers of the committee. . . .

Roused, the Commander summoned his supporters and protested in return against this attempt to set aside his authority. In reply the Commanders of the *Duchess* and the *Marquis* claimed to constitute a majority on the committee appointed by the owners, and as such appointed Captain Dover Commander of the new prize, renamed *Bachelor*, and served a formal, if ungrammatical, notification of the appointment upon Woodes Rogers.

We, thinking him the most proper person for the interests of the owners and company; we likewise propose to put two of the best of our officers on board to command under him and manage the navigation part of the voyage with other substantial officers and men, sufficient to watch the ship and take care of her.

The document ended with a formal protest against the Commander of the expedition, and declared him to be responsible for any loss of time, damage, or mutiny on the voyage home.

This was too much even for Woodes Rogers, patient and diplomatic though he had shown himself. In the interests of the expedition, "and being inclined to peace and quietness", he and his officers decided against any attempt to remove Dover forcibly from his position, "although he is utterly incapable of the office". But they put on record their emphatic and public protest against the appointment and all who had accepted it, and laid the entire responsibility on those who had put the prize under an incompetent commander.

By January 9th the dispute was still unsettled, and another meeting was held to which Woodes Rogers, still unable to attend because of his wounds, sent the following reasons why Dover should not be left in command of so valuable a ship.

He stated his opinion that it was not in the interest of the expedition that Captain Dover should command the "rich Spanish prize". Indeed, it would endanger her safety, not only because he was incapable, but because his temper was so violent that capable men could not well act under him. As to the claim that he should have no command over the actual direction of the ship, a commander needed many other qualifications than skill as a navigator. It was undesirable that anybody should take on so great a responsibility unless he was able to take on every part of it. Any attempt to split up the command must cause confusion, and in this case it would be "very pernicious".

Anxious if possible to reach a compromise, he added that he would be perfectly happy, indeed he would desire, to see Captain Dover aboard the prize, and with full leave and liberty to take care of the cargo; in fact, to do as he pleased, always provided that he were not in command.

A long debate followed, and finally agreement was reached. Mr. Fry and Mr. Stretton were voted as equal officers to take charge of the navigation under Captain Dover. He was, however, forbidden to molest, hinder, or contradict them in any decision they might see fit to take. It was, after all, his duty to act as an agent, and see that nothing should be done contrary to the interests of the owners and of the ship's company.

This in fact was almost what Woodes Rogers had at first proposed. The only difference was that Dover had the title of Chief Captain on board the prize. The title meant a good deal to him, and precious little to anybody else.

This memorandum sent to the committee by Woodes Rogers is the first open mention of Dover's violence of temper. There can be little doubt that it was justified. Although in one sense it comes from a hostile source, Woodes Rogers has painted an unconscious portrait of himself which shows that he was mild tempered, fair minded, and, in view of the many provocations he was given, both generous and forbearing.

Cooke's day-to-day entries, though far less detailed, on the whole confirm Woodes Rogers, but he tends on more than one occasion to take Dover's side. This he makes clear was less through love of Dover —though he says little in open criticism—than for reasons of policy and for his own convenience. In their accounts, both authors preserve a reticence remarkable in this vituperative age, and we are left to conjecture the details of many of the disputes from the bare outlines which have been recorded. Woodes Rogers shows the essence of the quarrels in a passage from his introduction, where he says that he would not have mentioned the matter, there or in his journal, "since the knowledge of our petty differences do no way concern the public", had not accounts of the whole matter been published already. He therefore felt himself obliged, in justice to his own reputation, and for the information of his friends, to set down his own account of the matter. Even so, he said as little about it as he could help, and "as softly as

IN MEMORY OF
ALEXANDER SELKIRK,
MARINER,
A NATIVE OF LARGO, IN THE COUNTY OF
FIFE, SCOTLAND.

WHO LIVED ON THIS ISLAND IN COM
PLETE SOLITUDE, FOR FOUR YEARS
AND FOUR MONTHS.

HE WAS LANDED FROM THE CINQUE
PORTS GALLEY, 96 TONS, 16 GUNS, A.D.
1704, AND WAS TAKEN OFF IN THE
DUKE, PRIVATEER, 12th FEB, 1709.

HE DIED LIEUTENANT OF H.M.S. WEY
MOUTH, A.D. 1723, AGED 47 YEARS.

THIS TABLET IS ERECTED
NEAR SELKIRK'S LOOKOUT, BY
COMMODORE POWELL AND THE
OFFICERS OF H.M.S. TOPAZE, A.D. 1868.

Picture Post

MEMORIAL PLAQUE TO ALEXANDER SELKIRK (*ROBINSON CRUSOE*

Dodd delinº   Page sculpº

A PIRATE hanged at Execution Dock.

Picture Post

A PIRATE HANGED AT EXECUTION DOCK

possible", keeping solely to matters of fact where he knew that no one of any substance could contradict him.

After all, as he points out, his was the main responsibility from the start of the expedition. Every resolution, every agreement made by the officers, was first proposed and drawn up by him. There was no power of compulsion, nor any rule to direct them, except the owners' instructions, and these were of such a nature that they could not always be adjusted to the unforeseen emergencies of the voyage. The reader, Woodes Rogers adds, may perhaps think he took too much upon him, since Dover was President of the Council and therefore had two voices. The reply to this was that though Dover had that office in the Council, in other respects he came third in command, according to the instructions laid down before the expedition set sail.

This is fair enough, the comment of a man with no love of recriminations, and preferring to let bygones be bygones. There were, however, further difficulties and provocations which do not come out in the open.

Woodes Rogers adds an ambiguous remark to his account of the events of the days spent at Grande Island. The letters to the owners, he says, contained all details of the voyage until that time.

. . . with two post-scripts wrote by Captain Dover and Captain Courtney, to put it out of doubt among those concerned, that we joined heartily in prosecuting our long understanding, and that our officers behaved themselves to satisfaction; which may clear up some difficulties started among the gentlemen at home before we sailed, that were a great hindrance and discouragement to us in the beginning, because mismanagement and misunderstanding among the officers never fail of ill effects on the voyage, and of spoiling the men, which is an irrecoverable loss.

What the difficulties were that had arisen even before the voyage neither he nor Cooke reveals; but it is clearly due to Woodes Rogers that the antipathies and grievances that were felt from the outset had not already developed into a state of intolerable friction. With the safety and success of the whole expedition depending upon the unanimity of the officers, Woodes Rogers was too experienced a Captain to exaggerate petty disputes, or to insist over-much on his authority over the other officers of the Council. He passes quietly over matters which a more vindictive character could have made much of, and writes with a dry dignity which, spread over his day-to-day account of three hazardous years, compels admiration and respect. His omission of personal grievances and self-justification convinces one that he was detached from the more petty interests of the other officers, and was often able to ignore the incidents when they occurred as deliberately as he omitted to enlarge upon them in his journal.

Occasionally he permits himself a complaint:

May 29, 1710 . . . A little before this, our Boat we had sent returned from the Shore, having by Presents engag'd a Canoe with some *Malayans* to come aboard with them, but for want of a *Linguist* we were little the better. I sent to the *Bachelor*, who had one, but Capt. *Dover* refus'd to let him come to me, altho' he had no use for him; then I sent a second Time, that I might know the best anchoring Place for our Ships, and treated the People (who were impatient to be gone) with Sweet-meats and other things they fancy'd, but could not keep 'em, or send them aboard the *Bachelor* to secure her, seeing white Shole-water near us. But they pass'd by us in danger of running on the Sholes, not knowing the best anchoring Place, for want of the Linguist I so earnestly desir'd, to understand the Malayans that had now left us.

III

The voyage home from California to Bristol then began. Woodes Rogers, sufficiently recovered to take command, led in the *Duke*. The *Duchess* was in charge of Courtney, the *Marquis* of Cooke, and the *Bachelor* of Dover.

The officers were granted a sum of money to refit themselves for the return journey. Dover was allowed 2000 pieces of Eight, Mr. Fry and Mr. Stretton 1000, Captain Cooke 800, Captains Rogers and Courtney 400, Dampier only 200, and three doctors on the *Duke*, the *Duchess*, and the *Marquis* a mere 90. There is no explanation of how these sums were arrived at.

For a few days the ships kept apart, and the atmosphere was sufficiently settled for Woodes Rogers to chronicle small matters in his journal. A boy named Thomas Conner fell overboard one morning. Luckily the launch was astern, so that a party of rescuers cut her moorings, and got to the boy just in time, as he was "tired with swimming and ready to sink".

What would have happened had the launch not been astern is not clear—except that the boy would probably have sunk anyway, since rescue would have been slower.

With each entry, Woodes Rogers's character comes out more clearly:

January 28th. The steward missing some pieces of pork, we immediately searched and found the thieves; one of 'em had been guilty before and forgiven on promise of amendment, but was punished now lest forbearance should encourage the rest to follow this bad practice. Provisions being so short, and our run so long, may prove of ill consequence. I ordered 'em to the main-gears and every man of the watch to give 'em a blow with the cat o' nine tails.

February 5th. A negro we named Debtford died, who being very much addicted to stealing of provisions, his room was more acceptable than his company at this time. . . . I shall only add that I found the character of the Hottentots to be very true and that they scarce deserve to be reckoned of the human kind, they are such ill-looked stinking nasty people. Their apparel is the skin of beasts, their chief adornment is to be very greasy and black, so that they besmear themselves with stinking oil or tallow and soot, and the women twist the guts of beasts or thongs of hides round their legs which resembles a tobacco roll.

By the middle of March, the bitterness between the rival factions had somewhat abated, chiefly because conditions were better, and because all were pleasantly eager to get home. On the Island of Guam, there was general merry-making and goodwill, Dover giving a party on the *Bachelor* for the "Spanish gentlemen", to which most of the officers were invited, and Woodes Rogers, still suffering from his wounds, was ceremonially hoisted aboard on a chair.

Gifts were added to hospitality—two negro boys dressed in livery, twenty yards of scarlet serge, and six pieces of cambric—in recognition of which the Englishmen were allowed to buy provisions for the journey home: twenty-two bullocks, six cows, sixty hogs, ninety-nine fowls, forty-four baskets of yams, twenty-four of Indian corn, fourteen of rice, and eight hundred coconuts.

The voyage through the Pacific was broken by calls at various islands, by provisioning at Bantam, Batavia, and Java, and by the usual hazards and accidents of a long voyage in those uncertain times. At Batavia, Cooke records:

The weather was extream hot during our Stay. Many Men and Officers fell sick, and I was one of the Number. The Master of the *Duke*, the Gunner of the *Duchess*, and several of our Men, dy'd of the Flux. John Read, a young Man belonging to the *Duchess*, venturing to swim, had both his Legs snapp'd off by a Shark, which at the second Bite, before we could get him aboard, took off the Bottom of his Belly, so that he was dead before we could take him up.

Disappointment and boredom at their slow progress revived the latent ill-will among the officers, and by the time they rounded the Cape of Good Hope, just after Christmas, they "could agree to nothing". Fortunately their disagreement did not lead to any kind of disaster, and on July the 23rd they landed in Holland.

The owners hastened across to learn the results of the voyage: but the formalities took a long time, and it was not till mid October that the ships came to anchor in the Downs, and, after three years at sea, Woodes Rogers was able thankfully to write:

"The end of our long and fatiguing voyage."

FOURTEEN

FROM the owners' point of view at any rate, the expedition was a great success. It seems that they were not ungenerous: Selkirk for his services as mate was paid £800. Woodes Rogers's share has nowhere been precisely stated, but Mr. G. E. Manwaring, in the introduction to his 1928 edition of the *Journal*, calculates it as in the neighbourhood of £14,000.

Still, after all expenses had been paid, there remained a profit of a hundred and seventy thousand pounds. We have no means of knowing how much of this went into Dover's pocket, but his share must have been considerable; enough to secure his independence in his profession for the rest of his life. He returned to Bristol, where his wife and children were awaiting him, and plunged back with renewed vigour into his medical work. The fame of the expedition was such that the three years' absence does not appear to have damaged his practice; and from this point on, as we shall see, he proceeded unswervingly on his own lines, with increasing scorn for those who differed from him.

His companions on the voyage disappear at once from our view. Dampier survived it by less than three years. Woodes Rogers enjoyed a period of retirement, during which he corresponded with such men as Addison, Steele, and Sir Hans Sloane. His journal of the voyage, supported as it is by Cooke's, shows him to have been an honest, steadfast, efficient, likeable man, who kept his dignity and his integrity in circumstances which would have made many men lose both. This in itself would be a sufficient epitaph; but there is more. What happened after his path diverged from Dover's is not strictly in our province, but it would be unfair to a remarkable man if there were no mention, however brief, of his subsequent achievements. In 1711, when the privateers reached the Cape of Good Hope, Rogers met some pardoned pirates who had been living until recently on Madagascar. He made in his journal a number of observations on the state of affairs in that island, which have not been recorded here because they have no bearing upon our main theme. Woodes Rogers followed the matter up, and, after the Treaty of Utrecht, he suggested

133

to the government that Madagascar should be colonized in order to prevent a revival of piracy there. There is no doubt that, if his advice had been taken, it would have saved the government and the East India Company a great deal of the trouble they were soon to meet.

Five years after his return he rented the Bahamas from the Lords Proprietors—the islands were privately owned at the time—at the same time obtaining a commission as Governor. Arriving in 1718, he found the islands a nest of pirates, and proceeded to offer pardon to any who surrendered before September 5th. Most of the pirates did surrender, and, aided mainly by a staff of Chelsea pensioners, Woodes Rogers formed a Council. Work was found for everyone. The ruined fort of Nassau was repaired, roads blocked with overgrown shrubs were cleared, and streets cleaned. Those who were not employed on this work were formed into companies of Militia, and Deputy Governors were appointed for the neighbouring islands. A scheme was devised to attract settlers to the province.

Unfortunately many of the pirates quickly tired of hard work, and escaped to return to their former way of life; and many settlers were found to be conspiring with them. Woodes Rogers wrote home for reinforcements, but the letters never arrived, and nothing was done. Finally, in despair, he returned to England in 1721. Here he met with almost as many difficulties, and could get no satisfaction. Another Governor was appointed in his place, but in 1728 a petition from the island pleaded for Woodes Rogers's return. In 1729 he sailed again for the Bahamas.

He stressed the necessity for the islands to be bought by the Crown, since there were continual struggles over the ownership of the land, so that constructive developments were impossible. He did not live to see his recommendations carried out, for he died in Nassau in 1732, and it was not until a year later that the Crown took over the land. His life there seems to have been a continuous battle against impossible circumstances, and only his strength of character and perseverance enabled him to establish the basis of an ordered community. It is probably not too much to say that he saved the Bahamas for Britain, and, more than anyone else, stamped out piracy in the Caribbean.

II

Dover spent five years in Bristol, consolidating his practice, and applying to the treatment of disease the principles he had learned from Dr. Sydenham, reinforced by his experience on the expedition and the conclusions he had drawn from it. In these years he began the lavish use of mercury for the treatment of a wide range of complaints, to which he owes his nickname of Dr. Quicksilver. This addiction, so soon after the voyage, may have been a mere coincidence, but I feel tempted to regard it as a consequence. The disorder for which it was a recognized specific is one which, on a voyage with shore calls at longish intervals, the ships' doctors would inevitably have to treat. We have already noted an instance of Dover's sardonic efficiency in the inclusion of an emetic in his famous powder. I think therefore that we may infer, without damage to probability, either that he was impressed by the general constitutional improvement in the men he treated, or that he attributed many of the disorders which took toll of the urban population to venereal disease of one kind or another. At all events, he dosed so many of his patients with mercury that the people of his day associated his name with nothing else.

Be this as it may, there is no doubt that, as a medical man, Dover learned a great deal from his voyage. For instance, in his comments on the widely prevalent "Green-sickness", he makes a common-sense remark supported by observations on his travels.

Since mothers have been so foolishly desirous for nice shapes for their children, and in their tender years have laced them so very strait that they have not only brought this distemper on more early, but caused great crookedness and deformity of the body . . . For these results one would think all mothers should become avowed enemies to lacing their daughters, till they are in their teens, at earliest, and not to act as if that wise being who made us in the womb, was ignorant how to model and shape us while we are growing to years of maturity. Let mankind take a view of barbarous countries as I have done; contemplate those people where God and Nature have only been; observe in what order and delicacy their muscles are placed; how strong their bodies, how taper their limbs. There are no full shoulders, no gummy thighs or legs, nor any deformity. . . .

This comment drew upon him the scorn of a number of his colleagues, whose explanations of the complaint were far more technical, and who did not at all welcome the idea of a preventive which might rob the profession of lucrative cases in the future. Some of the treatments they recommended were elaborate and costly. To suggest that the disease need not occur was the act of a blackleg.

The state of public health at the time when Dover was in practice is hard to determine at all accurately. There is plenty of evidence, but many of the figures are suspect and may be wildly wide of the mark. In the first place, there was a great deal of faulty diagnosis, due to a widespread ignorance of first principles. We can accept this even without what, coming from Dover, is a very temperate comment on the problem. With medicine in a sort of uneasy half-way house between the old magical outlook and the new attempts at objective observation and treatment, there was nothing platitudinous in what he had to say.

The first essential for the cure of any disease was, he stated baldly, a thorough acquaintance with its nature. Without this acquaintance no lasting good could be done, but a great deal of harm. The power of diagnosis could come only from experience, one's own, and that of other skilled physicians. Diagnosis was sometimes easy, but often very difficult. Such difficulty Dover ascribed to the "affinity and resemblance" between different diseases. Many diseases produced similar symptoms, but proceeded from entirely different causes. Thus the symptoms alone, unless they were most carefully examined and treated, might be misleading, and urge the physician to treat in the same way disorders which required entirely different treatment. For this reason it was necessary to study the patient as carefully as one studied the symptoms.

In complicated cases, "so very hard to be adjusted", the physician might be excused if he were sometimes a little wide of the mark. In simple diseases, a mistake admitted of no excuse.

Yet, even in "simple Diseases", there was abundance of error. Dover's ablest contemporaries support him here; and, even if they were not so explicit, numerous detailed records show that accurate diagnosis was a rarity, and appropriate treatment rarer still.

Another source of error was that the "official searchers", whose business it was to ascertain and record the cause of death, were frequently bribed to enter false reports. This is acknowledged in the edition of Stow's *Survey of London*, which had been "corrected and improved, and very much enlarged" by John Strype in 1720, and was reissued in a sixth edition in 1755, "brought down to the present time by careful hands".

The figures given by these "careful hands" can at best be a reasonable guess; but they are all we have, and may be quoted with this caution.

The one certain fact was that the death rate was terribly high. Strype and Co. estimate the population of London at 186,000, with an avowed death rate of 28,000. Of these 10,000 belonged to children under two years old, and a further 2,500 to children under five. It is significant here that, in all his account of forty-nine years' practice,

Dover never once mentions treating a small baby. The inference would seem to be that little was done to reduce the appallingly high rate of infant mortality.

If this was so, the latter part of the century brought a change. An anonymous work, published in 1776, in Dublin, and entitled *The Modern Family Physician, or the Art of Healing Made Easy*, tells a very different story. I shall return to it in a minute or two, for its common-sense attitude and its attention to minor as well as major illness shows the tremendous advances made in sixty or seventy years, and those advances prove that the attitude towards medicine of Sydenham, Radcliffe, and Dover had prevailed. The dust of the ridiculous controversies had settled, and the clear lines of the new science were beginning to emerge.

But to return to London. In the immense annual death-roll recorded by Strype and his helpers, 8,000, he said, died of "convulsions"; "fevers and consumptions" took off 4,000 each, smallpox 2,000: "from all of which it appears that London is not an unhealthy place".

These spectacular diseases were the chief foes Dover had to fight, and we shall presently see, from his own records, how he set about them. Violence was the basis of most of the treatment, violence proportionate to that of the disease: but the objective method which Dover taught bore fruit for his immediate successors, and, as the Dublin physician's book attests, led to a more realistic and reasonable approach and to a greater reliance on the patient's natural powers of resistance and recuperation.

First of all comes the greater interest in the health of children. The anonymous author writes at length about the particular diseases that children suffered from, and the best treatment in each case. More remarkably he lays down rules for the general upbringing of children, stressing the importance of light comfortable clothing, a maximum of freedom for movement, regular and simple food, fresh air, cleanliness, and other principles we might not expect to find till a much later date. But this is fifty years after the days when Dr. Dover was practising in Bristol, and is, besides, the work of a man whose remedies could be as effectively followed today as in the eighteenth century. He pointed out that the terrible prevalence of disease among the working people would only be remedied when the causes were removed, and that the ill-health of the poor was due to bad food, dirt, overwork, inadequate or unsuitable clothing, and ignorance of the most elementary rules of health. The diseases from which studious and learned people suffered were caused by too much exertion of the brain, too little physical exercise, and sitting up late at night. Stuffy rooms, falling asleep after dinner, and too much tobacco aggravated their unhealthiness. The anonymous doctor recommended instead plenty of riding, walking, skittles, bowling, and hunting, and a light diet of milk, eggs, and fresh fruit, with a minimum of rich food, particularly of fried dishes and cocoa. Watering-places were, he said, valuable for the minerals, but in the case of studious gentlemen, even more valuable because:

. . . they serve to wear off much of that rust which literary men contract in their studies, and make them much better members of human society than all the books in the world ever could. For study is only one part of learning.

He deals at length with nervous diseases, and particularly with low-ness of spirits, which he says is often the result of contemplating too much the affairs of human life, and from imaginary fears.

Some are naturally subject to lowness of spirit, but by far the greatest number of those who are afflicted by it are those who seclude themselves from society, and spend their time in solitude. A Gothic structure, or an ancient grove in a wood equally promote all the effects of this disorder, and from that circumstance alone we may learn that man was formed for society. . . . Peace of mind, and a fixed tranquillity under all dispensations of providence will preserve the body from many diseases, especially such as arise from many disorders of the senses.

On the subject of tea this anonymous author is cautious; he admits that it may be prejudicial to the nerves if taken excessively, as it was so often adulterated by the time it reached England:

But this prejudice against tea may be carried too far, for if it is genuine, it may safely be drunk, except too much be taken at one time. If a person finds his nerves disordered after drinking tea, and if his hand shakes; if he is seized with a giddiness in the head, and a dejection of spirits, he may be assured that it does not agree with him.

The other point to note about this book, apart from its reasonable-ness, is the absence of the vituperative note which envenoms almost all of Dover's pronouncements. However quiet and sensible in themselves, they nearly always have a sting in the tail, when he turns to contrast his own enlightened procedure with the obtuse or demented practices of his opponents.

This was especially unfortunate, as it delayed the acceptance of his views and prejudiced the rest of the medical profession against them. The opposition which he roused was due not so much to his medical theories as to his aggressive presentation of them, and his vilification of all who did not agree. Still, as the Dublin doctor's book proves for us, good sense prevailed.

III

After more than five years' practice in Bristol, Dover moved to London. We have not the exact date of his move, but before the end of 1717 he was visited in Cecil Street by a patient whom he had cured of what other physicians had pronounced to be an incurable gout.

In 1721 the name of Thomas Dover appears on the roll of the Royal College of Physicians. Dr. D. N. Phear has shown that he was examined three times, in Physiology, Pathology, and Therapeutics. On the first occasion he asked for a postponement, as he had not yet received his M.B. Diploma from Cambridge. Appearing with it on May 5th, he was successful and completed the examinations in July. Finally, on the proposal of Sir Hans Sloane, he was admitted on September 30th, but had to wait till the next Comitia for his Diploma to be sealed, as the key had been lost. From then until his withdrawal into Gloucestershire, he lived the leisured and well-graced life of an eighteenth-century Londoner in comfortable circumstances. His favourite haunt was the Jerusalem Coffee House. Here he gave his consultations, had his prescriptions brought by the apothecaries, and his letters delivered. His range of patients was widely varied, making it obvious that he took some out of sheer interest in their condition. They range from the coachman mentioned on p. 150 to "gentlemen of reputation and figure", including worthies from Russell Street and a Chancery clerk of Furnival's Inn, residing near Hampton Court.

He got into hot water with the College of Physicians quite soon after his admission, for taking over another doctor's patient without consulting him. Dover denied all knowledge of this Dr. Wagstaffe, but "was admonished". There were also complaints that he broke the College's rule that a doctor should not tell his patients the names of any medicines. But these were trifling matters in comparison with the controversies he was presently to arouse.

We have no exact date for Dover's withdrawal into the country, but it must have been before 1728, since he was actively engaged in dealing with the epidemics which raged there in that year and in 1729. In choosing Gloucestershire he was returning to that part of England where he had spent his childhood. Probably he spent the years away from London at Stanway, the fine house of his mother's family, the Tracys: and it was to John Tracy that he dedicated *The Ancient Physician's Legacy*. If indeed he stayed with the Tracys, it was as a friend rather than as a physician; the financial aspect of his profession never seems to have caused him any anxiety.

He returned to London somewhere about the beginning of 1732, and was there when the book was published a year later, starting the spate of controversy through which his name was chiefly known.

FIFTEEN

*T*HE *Ancient Physician's Legacy to his Country* is Dover's testament. It contains his medical beliefs, his account of the diseases he met with, and of how he treated them. It also tells us something about the man himself—though not nearly as much as a biographer could wish.

The fact that emerges most vividly, once again, is that Dover's professed and strong design to help mankind was retarded by the belligerence with which he advanced his own beliefs and repudiated those of others. That he thought highly of his profession and was zealous for its ethical principles appears sufficiently from his introduction. There is an unmistakable thread of benevolence running through the pattern of the book, obscured from time to time by outbursts of impatience and irritation against those who did not at once acknowledge the correctness of the advocate's conclusions. Reading between the lines, we may be thankful that the powerful influence of Sydenham inclined his pupil along the right path, and saved him from advocating, with even greater venom, worse prescriptions.

To say this is not to belittle Dover, but to be glad that his vehemence and obstinacy were directed into sound channels by the example of a man whose greatness he always acknowledged. That he was no mere follower we see in his frank dissent from Sydenham where his own experience pointed to better methods of treatment: the difference being that from Sydenham he dissented respectfully and without vainglory, giving chapter and verse for his opinion.

This is important, because it shows that Dover had the scientific attitude. His first devotion was to medicine. Facts were sacred. We can see that he did not always live up to his principles. The remarkable thing is that, being the man he was and living when he did, he had such principles. That fact alone would put him in a high class and ensure him an honourable place in medical history.

II

His book, then, is worth looking at in detail. I shall quote from it freely, rather than paraphrase, since Dover's own words reveal the man. The book appeared with the following title-page:

The Ancient Physician's Legacy to his Country. Being what he has collected himself in forty nine years practice:
or
An account of the several diseases incident to Mankind, described in so plain a manner, that any person may know the nature of his own disease. Together with the several remedies for each distemper faithfully set down. Designed for the use of all private families.
Homines ad Deos, nulla in re proprius accedunt, quam salutem hominibus dando. Cic:
By Thomas Dover. M.B.   London.
Printed for the author: And sold by A. Bettesworth and C. Hitch, in Pater-Noster Row; W. Mears at the 'Lamb' in the Old Bailey; and Lawton Gulliver at Homer's Head, over against St. Dunstan's Head, Fleet Street, 1732.
Price Stitched. Five Shillings.

The dedication to John Tracy Esq., of Stanway in Gloucestershire, sounded a strong and slightly cantankerous note.

Amidst the general corruption into which we are fallen, Physick has not preserved its purity; though this is perhaps too important a truth to be published with safety. There is a craft (if the word is not too harsh) in this profession, as well as in all others, and the greatest part of its followers will not fail to oppose the least step towards a Reformation.

Your reputation is so well established, that the sheltering myself under your name may be some security against calumny; your esteem must naturally secure me the esteem of all good men; and this one would think might soften, if not entirely subdue the spirit of detraction.

To mention the antiquity of your family, though it extends to the most ancient of our Kings, is needless: your own personal merit gives you a much higher value, not only than your birth, but than any title which the crown could confer upon you. I have ever hated flattery and I believe there is not a gentleman who has the honour and happiness to know you, but will readily allow that what I say is strictly true.

Could this essay as effectively establish the health as the whole course of your life has promoted the happiness of mankind, it would more than answer my utmost hopes. But however short I may fall in this respect, I have at least the opportunity of gratifying my ambition, by declaring myself, Sir, Your most obliged, most faithful, and most

> devoted servant,
> Thomas Dover.

In the introduction which follows Dover explains that his only reason for publishing his observations is his desire to benefit mankind. The same mixture of self-confidence and defensiveness colours the statement of his purpose.

My design is to touch on such parts of Physick, as I conceive most necessary to be understood by every Practitioner, and which seem to me hitherto to have been neither explained, nor accounted for in a proper Manner, notwithstanding the voluminous Works in which they have been treated of.

Authors for the most Part follow one another, and deviate but little from the common Track. This Method I shall in no wise pursue; my Design being to set down only such Things as have occurred to me from the Practice and Experience of forty nine years. I am very sensible that my Stile is not correct, and I shall take no extraordinary Care to polish it. I shall be sufficiently satisfied, if what I write be thought worth attending to.

He would like to deserve the comment made by Mr. Budgell on the writing of Mr. Boyle:

Under all these disadvantages, so curious is his matter and so solid are his observations that the barest thing we can say of his most careless piece is, that it appears like a beautiful woman in undress.

This strange aspiration is hardly fulfilled. Budgell was a queer model, his main claim to fame being a mention in the *Dunciad*:

> Let Budgell charge low Grub Street on his quill,
> And write whatse'er he please—except his will.

and another, no more complimentary, in *The Rehearsal*:

> Poet Budgell came next, and, demanding the bays,
> Said those works must be good which had Addison's praise;
> But Apollo replied: Child Eustace, 'tis known
> Most authors will praise whatsoever's their own.

The encomium of Boyle is obscure, even from such a source. Difficult though it is to see what Budgell was driving at, the terms "curious" and "solid" being equivocal in connection with beauty in undress, we can safely say that Dover's style does not live up to the tribute. The matter is solid and curious enough, but there is nothing feminine in its presentation.

Dover then lays down the principles on which he has practised medicine:

It is essentially necessary in the cure of diseases, to be thoroughly acquainted with the nature of them. Without this knowledge no good is to be done.

Rigorous examination, questioning, and observation are necessary before any attempt to prescribe.

Instead of giving us such necessary preliminaries, many lay the whole stress of curing diseases upon the number of their receipts, stuffing their books with long and tedious prescriptions; which is little better than teaching us how to cure people, before we know the nature of their distemper.

Jargon and mystification are quite unnecessary. Instead,

I hope to describe the most common (Diseases) in so plain a manner that even the patient himself shall be able to give a plain and proper name to his disease.

He is quite confident in his own judgment, but, in spite of his declarations that he is well used to criticism and untroubled by it, he attacks in advance anyone whom he believes may differ from him. Before he settles down to describe specific ailments and their treatment, there are things to be said about doctors and about medicine in general. He sharply condemns the young physicians who went abroad to gain experience which did not always prove to be medical:

The late famous Dr. Radcliff was of Opinion, That it was expedient for young Gentlemen, entering upon our Profession, to travel; and that such as pursued their Studies at Home, could not (allowing they have had the Advantages of an academical education) improve themselves equally with those that spend many years Abroad and make good use of their Time. . . .

Perhaps he had done better, if he had obliged those Gentlemen to practice Physick, at least ten Years, before their setting out for foreign

NORTH-WEST PROSPECT OF BRISTOL IN 1734

JOHN RADCLIFFE

Parts: They would then have been much more capable of making such Observations, as might be of singular Use to them: and 'tis farther my Opinion, That if he had ordered them to visit most intemperate Climates, where all the acute Diseases are most violent, they would have returned Masters of greater Knowledge and Experience, than they can ever acquire by only passing through the most healthy Parts of Europe, which seems more like travelling for the sake of their own Health, than that of other people.

If travelling be necessary to make an accomplished Physician, I am very sure that I have travelled more than all the Physicians in Great Britain put together.

But I am going a little out of my way. . . .

The book is not made easier reading by the many occasions on which he shows an old man's tendency to digress:

. . . I beg my Reader's Pardon for so long a Digression; but I hope, the importance of the Subject will sufficiently atone for it. I can assure them, what has been said on this Occasion, is not from any view to my own private interest, but merely out of Regard to the general Good of Mankind.

He comes out as a strong believer in nature and her *vis medicatrix*, her tendency to find a cure.

Nature will neither be forced nor driven, and is often very hard to be led; but will do wonders when properly assisted.

He believes that purges are better than vomiting, since nature intended anything taken in at the mouth to pass through the body. Forcing it up again is "a contrary Motion, which is too great a strain for those fine Vessels, by which Means they become lax, and are much weakened . . ."

If a bird or a dog is ill, it finds its own remedy, bathing in cold water, or eating some particular kind of grass. Yet if a human being is ill, he is denied the things which his instinct demands.

This is contradicting the Rules of Nature, and must certainly be wrong. Right Reason, and the Rules of Nature, will eternally tally.

Another detail in which he was ahead of his time is his belief in the value of eating raw fruit:

The reader must pardon a short Digression: Since mention has been made of Mothers, I can't but observe, how religiously they restrain their Children from eating green Fruit, from a Notion that it breeds worms. However singular I may appear in my Opinion, I hold the contrary to be true; green Fruit being rather a great Destroyer of Vermin.

'Tis Ripe Fruits that breed Worms. . . .

This belief in natural cures leads him to suspect drugs:

. . . no Body can have the Gout to that Degree, but that there may be a Rebate given to his Pains. He may find great Relief without Opiates, or painful Remedies, which I am a Stranger to, and very much dislike;

and he looks upon medicine altogether as a matter of common sense. Where he thinks this quality is lacking, he lays about him.

'Tis surprising to me that Physicians can read so many authors, and overlook the most reasonable Rules for the Good and Preservation of mankind, and imbibe Principles, which, were it not for fear of giving Offence, I should say, are contrary to Common Sense.

This sudden "fear of giving offence" may suggest that in his old age he was less vehement and hasty than he appears to have been in his younger days. More likely he was being sarcastic, a faculty which had not left him.

After the learned Dr. Willis has made a very long Harangue about hot Scurvy and cold Scurvy, I must own my Capacity too weak to comprehend his Meaning; nor do I believe the Disease owed its Name to any Thing, but that When the Physicians met with a Distemper they knew little of, they called it a scurvy one.

A great deal of the book is taken up with descriptions of the symptoms of the various diseases as Dover saw them, and the treatment which he followed, substantiated with case histories. Among the diseases he writes about are dropsy, gout, scurvy, consumption, diabetes, asthma, rheumatism, plague, leprosy, smallpox, measles, fevers in general, erysipelas, pleurisy, and quinsy. Sometimes we get less about Dover's treatment than we do about the alleged mistreatment by other doctors.

Sometimes his own treatment was open to attack. It is difficult to see what medical philosophy or experience inspired his treatment for asthma: "a Toad dried and powdered, made into Pills, and taken as above, is a most excellent Remedy". There follows an almost equally curious comment:

But we are so wise as to take it for granted that a Toad is a very poisonous Animal: Our Mothers instill into us such an Aversion against the poor innocent and harmless Creature, that whenever we see him, most certainly he is stoned to Death: Whereas, rightly considered, he is a very great Blessing bestowed on Mankind.

Still, the treatment was evidently successful, as evidenced by the case of Miss Corbet already quoted, and that of Mr. William Staunton, the former Chancery clerk of Furnival's Inn, who was afflicted for twenty years with vehement asthma, and had recourse to doctor after doctor, until he followed Dover's treatment and was cured.

Consumption called forth violent differences of opinion with other doctors, including, as we have already seen, one from Sydenham, who recommended riding. Dover's remedies were based upon bleeding, fresh air, and cold water. He starts off by attacking current medical belief. Physicians, he knows, have often claimed that immersion in cold water has caused consumptions.

If they can make this appear from one single instance, it may give some satisfaction as to what they assert, though it will be far from proving their conclusion to be true. What they say of cold bathing is very different from what I have experienced in practice, and from my way of thinking. I have dealt upon this head because I would have cold bathing show as universal as I hope inoculation in a short time will do.

Cold bathing, incidentally, was one of Dover's panaceas. He mentions it in many connections, including his note on leprosy. "The Israelites," he says, "were famous for an itchy, scabby people, and the only remedy they made use of, was immersion in cold water."

But to return to consumption. In his comments on this, Dover raises the difficulty of strengthening the patient without also giving food to the disease.

As this is an inflammatory Disease, all Methods of Cure ought to be avoided, except such as abate the Inflammation; which, I may venture to say, is usually increased by the vast quantities of Oils and Syrups prescribed: and this is the Chief Reason that Physicians have had so little Success in Consumptions. They allow the Patient to use a strengthening Diet, and indulge him too much with Wine, Gravies, and the like, contrary to a known Maxim in Physick—*Impura corpora quo plus nutries, eo magis laedes.* . . .

One Mr. William Masters, an eminent Surgeon at Evesham, in Worcestershire, was so far gone in a Consumption, that he was not able to stand alone. I advised him by all Means to lose six Ounces of Blood every Day for a Fortnight, if he lived so long; then every other day, then every third day, and fifth day for the same Time. This was in the Month of November. The March following, he rode from Evesham to Bristol in one Day, which is forty seven Miles, to give me thanks for his recovery—he lived many Years after. His relations all died in Consumptions. This was the first Experiment I made of Bleeding in this Disease; and have cured many since by the same Method.

It is interesting to see, as it were in embryo form, the perplexities that have worried the medical profession since doctors first became aware of them. Though, as we shall presently see, Dover came to look on mercury as a panacea, he was anything but rigid in his views about other prescriptions and expedients. He advocates bleeeding in all fevers, from smallpox to measles, but is far from looking upon it as useful in every disease.

Bleeding in Convulsions, if it has not been, ought to be exploded; and in Fulness, occasioned by Dropsies, it is pernicious to the last Degree. . . .

The fluids in the human body Dover regarded as "the seat of all distempers", maintaining that the solid parts were only passive, and complaining that not enough attention had been given to this important distinction, although it was "of so great use in the art of healing".

By his own account he was very successful with cases of dropsy, but complained that as a rule he only got patients suffering from it when they had despaired of other physicians, or other physicians had despaired of them. Even so, he claims to have saved many lives, with an acerbity which was one of the main causes of the book's unpopularity with the medical profession as a whole. Sometimes the unsuccessful physicians were named, occasionally with a compliment which must have struck them as left-handed.

Another patient had a white swelling as the Surgeons call it, in both knees. He came to Town, and applied himself to Mr. Bocheer who like an honest man did little to him, but advised him to go to Bath which he did for near twenty years, as the Gentleman told me. But in the end this proved to be an Ascites. I was called to him; and upon purging off the waters, those white swellings completely disappeared. He told me he had not had so good a command of his legs for twenty years past.

He criticizes a method of treatment that long outlived him.

I am surprised that a Paracentesis or Tap should be so frequently used in this fatal Disease and I should be glad to know if one in five hundred has been cured by it. It rather confirms the Disease, and often renders it incurable, while the poor Patient's Life is protracted in Misery and Despair . . .

Another reference to rival physicians occurs in a case of Anasarca, a kind of dropsy, "not so common as the Ascites, or Tympany", but "much easier cured". The patient was a Mr. Towne, one of the King's gardeners, and the physician the celebrated Dr. Radcliffe. Dover was called to the patient in his extremity, but

. . . the Doctor was so confident of saving him by the wonderful Panacaea Blisters, that I was not listened to. The Blisters, instead of proving Remedies, only gave the Patient Pain, without affording him any Help; so that in a short Time after he died.

The remedy Dover would have given is interesting:

Take Steel prepared with Sulphur and crude Antimony, each one Ounce, Diagridium four Ounces; Make a fine Powder of these; then add as much of any Syrup as will make a soft Electuary—take a large Spoonful at night going to Bed, and another in the Morning, stirring it well from the Bottom, increasing or lessening the Dose as you see Occasion—You must not drink during the Operation of this Physick, as in other Purges; for if you pour in too much Liquor, it will destroy the End of Purging, and you will find yourself just where you were.

When your waters are off, you may repeat your Purge once in four or five Days; then once a Week, and so on, to once a Fortnight, and once a Month, till your Blood has recovered its due Tone.

You must avoid all Spoon-Meats, Fruits, and Garden-stuff, of what kind soever—and be sure not to exceed a Pint and a half of Liquor in twenty four Hours; for if you drink, your Thirst will never abate. By this method, and God's Blessing, I have cured Hundreds in my time.

He dismisses a little more modestly the attempts which previous physicians have made to cure gout:

There have been so many unsuccessful Attempts to master this Disease, that Patients have very little Faith left, and (as they commonly say) have no Hopes from any Thing but Patience and warm Flannel: But with Submission, keeping the Part warm is wrong, because 'tis *proprium Caloris attrahere*; and does, beyond doubt, attract Gouty Matter to the Part. . . .

This painful disease is one of the occasions on which Dover shows that he thought of his patients as human beings, not merely as cases, or a source of income. Gout "takes its Progress increasing by Degrees, till the poor Patient is lacerated, and torn to Pieces . . .".

After details of the onset of a typical case, Dover refers to Providence, with the implication that he has been privileged often to be its agent.

. . . A regular Gout may most properly be termed Podagra, because it begins in the first Joint of the Great Toe, and that usually about Midnight; where, after it has rack'd the Patient forty eight Hours with a violent fix'd Pain, a small Tumour begins to appear. . . .

Providence has in this, as well as in all other Diseases, left Means for our recovery, which in many Instances I am able to make appear . . . The Coachman of the Right Honourable the Lord Viscount St. John had a long and tedious fit of the Gout, and was hardly able to stir without Crutches. I gave him a very pleasant easy Sudorific, which had its desired Effect:— insomuch that the Day following, he walked from Albemarle Street to Cecil Street, to give me thanks. He came to me without the Help of a Stick, and with strait Shoes: The Swelling was entirely gone: He affirmed that he was never better in his Life; and that he was able to walk from one End of the Town to the other. This is about fifteen Years ago.

The Fellow has never had any return since, though he was much afflicted with it many years before—it may be asked, Will he never have it again? The same Question may be asked of any Fever (except some few with Eruptions) for many Persons are very subject to Fevers every Spring; yet I presume no Body will say a Patient was not cured of a Fever he had fifteen Years since, though he should happen to have a Fever again this Year.

For fevers in general, Dover placed great reliance on bleeding, maintaining that it saved many a life which other physicians had despaired of—as in the case of Miss Corbet, already referred to on p. 64. He also recommended it in cases of erysipelas, pleurisy, quinsy, and the plague. In his dissertation on smallpox he professes that he cannot understand the attitude taken by other medical men:

It must be want of observation that makes Physicians so fearful of bleeding in this distemper after the eruption. The good Dr. Sydenham goes no further than *Mittetur sanguis quovis die ante tertium* inclusive, which is but the second day of their appearances. But the most excellent Peter Beyrus of Turin, who wrote about one hundred and ninety years since, goes further; and I can affirm by experience, and from the success I have had, that the patient may be blooded every, or any day to the twenty-first.

"I am credibly informed," he goes on, "that the most learned and ingenious Dr. Boerhaave, in all fevers bleeds plentifully, gives air to his patient immediately, tears off all blisters, and indulges the sick person with all manner of cooling and diluting liquors."

His treatment is, he admits, unorthodox, but he claims that it has nevertheless been so effective as to be preferred to the treatment recommended by learned theorists who base all their knowledge on books and make no concessions to experience. As an example of successful treatment he quotes an occasion when he was in Gloucestershire at the time of a fever epidemic.

I am very sensible, my Method in curing Fevers, is much exploded, because I act quite contrary to the common Practice. I happened to live in Gloucestershire, in the years 1728 and 1729; when a very fatal Epidemical Fever raged to such a degree, as to sweep off whole Families, nay, almost whole villages. I was called to several Houses, where eight or nine Persons were down at a time; and yet did not so much as lose one Patient where I was concerned. I defy the Malice of my most implacable Enemies to make it appear that in my ten Years last Practice, I have lost twelve Patients in all kinds of Fevers put together.

I do not seek applause for this performance, especially from the gentlemen of the faculty, being sensible how many great and powerful enemies I have amongst them. Who, as they have done all they could hitherto to discredit my practice, so probably will take occasion from the publication of these sheets, to improve their invectives and resentment against me. But as custom has made ill-usage familiar to me, I think I am prepared for any future calumny. In the meantime I would caution any unwary people against one thing; which is, not to mistake every graduate for a physician, nor a clan of prejudiced gentlemen for oracles. Experience is all in all; and I will venture to say some experience has fallen to my share, having sought it in other places besides the shops of Apothecaries, or the Colleges of Physicians.

The conclusion is characteristic. There is a quality in Dover which, even at his most truculent, attracts one's sympathies as he attacks this "clan of prejudiced gentlemen" and presents his case to the tribunal of the public. His object in writing his experiences was, he said, simply to benefit mankind with the observations of forty-nine years:

If this should not be allowed as a sufficient reason by some who have expressed no good-will towards me, it will give me but little concern: I leave what I write to the unprejudiced reader.

All the same, he got a great deal of fun out of trouncing his many opponents.

The case histories he gives are striking and circumstantial. For example:

The Case of John Dineley Goodeere, Esq. of Charlton in Worcestershire, near Evesham, was very remarkable: Some Years ago, when he was in London, he was seized with a violent Fever. He was unwilling that Sir Edward Goodeere, his Father, who was in Town at the same Time, should know any Thing of it; so that he was, as it were, in Extremis before his father was acquainted with it. He ordered me immediately to be called to his Son; whose Eyes were set in his Head, his Jaw fallen, his Tongue directly black and hard, his Face as black as an Indian, with Drops upon it as big as Pease or Pulse. The Apothecary being present, I asked him if he blooded. He told me, Yes; and accordingly got every Thing in order for it. I bid him take Care to make a large Orifice, which he did. He asked me how much Blood he must take away. I answered I could not tell. He said he had taken twelve Ounces. I said, Let the Patient bleed on. The Apothecary now told me he had drawn twenty Ounces. Then I discerned something of a Pulse coming on in my patient. In the Conclusion, he bled to forty eight or fifty Ounces. The Sweat went off, and his Face came to its Colour. Whilst he was bleeding, I got a cool Tankard of Rhenish Wine, Water, and Lemon, which held near three Quarts: I raised him upon his Pillow, and gave him about a Pint-Glassful; and immediately after he began to move his Eyes, and close his Jaws. In a very short Time after, I gave him a couple of Glasses more. He then fixed his Eyes hard upon me, put his Hand out to me, and said, Is it you, my dear Friend? I asked him, If he could drink. He answered, The Ocean. I made those about him rub his Head with dry Clothes, and then asked how he found himself. He answered, In a strange confused Condition. In one Hour, or thereabouts, he flung the Clothes off the Bed, put his Feet in his Slippers, called for his Night-Gown, walked to the other side of the Room, set himself down in a two-armed Chair, Now, my dear Friend, (says he) we will have one Flask of Claret together. I told him, I would drink a Flask of Claret; but that he must stick to his Cool Tankard.

The next Morning, when I came to wait on him, he was down in the Stable amongst his Horses, without a Cap, having nothing on but his Night-Gown and Slippers. I asked him, how he did? He said, Never better in all his Life. This was in the Month of March.

III

Dover puts scarlet fever down as being milder than measles, passing in forty-eight hours, and dismisses chicken-pox as something which does not need a doctor. Quinsy, on the other hand, may easily kill in eight hours.

Children with Anomalous Small Pox:

. . . never salivate, but for a Diarrhoea or Looseness, which is much the same in effect. Where the Physician stops it, he kills the Child; and how many poor Babes have lost their Lives by this Practice, 'tis terrible to Think.

Of measles he takes occasion to say:

I do not remember I ever heard anyone dying of this disease till about twenty years hence; but of late, by the help of Gascoyne's Powder and Bezoartic Bolusses, together with Blisters and a hot regimen, which if practised on a healthy person would endanger his life, the blood is so high enflamed and the fever increased so to that degree, that it is become equally mortal with the small-pox.

The "Bezoartic Bolusses" ran neck and neck with Gascoyne's Powder as quarry for Dover's derisive shafts. He will hear no good of either. In another place he lists the powder among the killers—"the so much celebrated Gascoyne Powder, which occasions yearly the loss of so many subjects to the crown". With satisfaction he gives us his own account of the exploit on the cruise, related already by Woodes Rogers. On board ship a hundred and eighty men contracted the plague from the Spaniards. Dover had them all bled, and gave them oil, spirit of vitriol and water to drink freely, and "only seven or eight died", whereas the Spaniards lost a great many men. (Woodes Rogers—*see* Appendix D—gives the number as eleven.)

Now if we had had Recourse to Alexipharmicks, such as Venice Treacle, Diacordium, Mithridate, and such like good-for-nothing Compositions, or the most celebrated Gascoyne's Powder, or Bezoar, I make no question at all, considering the Heat of the Climate, but we had lost every Man.

Bezoar, for which Dover expressed equal contempt, was a stone from the stomach of certain wild animals. He calls it:

. . . that petrified Matter of Disease, cut out of the Paunches, Galls, and Bladders of some of the nastiest Creatures in being, as Guananoes, a monstrous Beast between a Camel and a He-Goat, black Cattle, Hogs, Goats, and an ugly animal they call Pacos de la Tierra, Monkeys, Porcupines, and all such nasty animals. . . . We, in Dissections, too often find in the Galls and Bladders of Human Bodies great quantities of Stones, which doubtless may as well serve for Bezoar as the diseased matter of the afore-mentioned Beasts.

Small wonder that his colleagues resented these comments on their favourite remedies.

Blistering, too, he attacks again and again :

One would think from the new-invented Way of curing this Distemper (Flux Small-Pox) by Blistering . . . that this Disease must certainly bring its Remedy with it; for here is a Blister from Head to Foot, and consequently this Confluent Kind of Small Pox ought to be less dangerous than the other two Sorts. But to our great Grief, we find this Sort to be more difficult to be cured. . . .

In dealing with scurvy, his tone is once more contemptuous :

There needs nothing more to be done for the Cure of this Disease, which has hitherto puzzled Physicians in all Ages, than to drink a quarter of a Pint of Allom Posset-Drink, first and last, made as strong as your stomach will bear it—This I have experienced for thirty-five Years, and do not remember that it ever failed.

He is distressed that medicine is able to do so little for sick people :

Paracelsus . . . very much recommends the inner Bark of Barberries, Turmerick, Rheubarb, and all Plants of a yellow Cast, in the cure of this Disease (Jaundice). But they are too weak . . . I mention this, to show on what weak Foundations we often venture our Lives.

. . . At the Bath, I have seen gentlemen so far gone in this Disease, that their Faces have been of an exact Lemon-Colour—I have been much concerned, to think how small a Progress has been made in the Art of Healing.

The implication is, almost always, that such advance as has been made is due to him and a few who think as he does.

About thirty seven Years since this Fever (spotted) raged much in Bristol, so that I visited from twenty five to thirty Patients a day for a considerable Time, besides their poor Children taken into their Workhouse, where I engaged myself, for the Encouragement of so good a charitable Undertaking, to find them Physick, and give them Advice at my own Expence and Trouble for the two first Years. All these poor Children in general had this Fever, yet no more than one died out of the whole Number, which was over two hundred.

He gives his patients credit for a certain amount of sense:

I must give the Reader one Caution, That there is a great Difference in the several Constitutions of Mankind; and therefore it must be left to every man's Discretion, as to the Quantity he is to take of each of these Medicines, . . .

though, as we have seen, he has little to say in favour of mothers who have more care for their daughters' figures than for their health.

He proclaims that women

. . . are of a much finer Texture of Body than Men, they are more subject to the Passions of the mind, which have often been the Cause of this Distemper (Tympany—a type of dropsy).

and even in his old age he is susceptible to female charm:

I would have Cold Bathing grow as universal, as I hope, Inoculation in a short time will do. And now I have mentioned inoculation, I should think it unpardonable if I should take no Notice of Her Majesty as a great Promoter and Encourager of this Practice . . . Inoculation is as beneficial an Invention, in every Respect, as either this Age, or any of the preceding ones have produced. Yet, what is very surprising, it meets with little Encouragement from the Ladies. Is Beauty, that arrives at such a Perfection in an English Climate, of so little Importance, that it is beneath our Care? . . . The Ladies may possibly smile to hear a Man of Seventy use such warm Expressions, but I will venture to say with Mr. Dryden that

> Old as I am, for Ladies Love unfit,
> The Power of Beauty I remember yet.

I therefore lament the small and inconsiderable Progress which Inoculation has as yet made in Great Britain.

As to that ridiculous aspersion some people have cast on it, by calling it a tempting of God, and bringing diseases upon ourselves: this to a thinking person must appear so frivolous, that it scarcely deserves an answer. Is there one single passage in the whole Sacred writings, that restrains Mankind from anticipating an evil, by making use of proper precautions for preventing it? If these scrupulous gentlemen, whose consciences were not always so strait-laced, will produce me but one single instance of an absolute prohibition from things of this nature, I will readily acquiesce, and willingly retract my error.

Another rather odd comment on women appears in the paragraphs on Hemiplegie:

The great Author of Nature has afforded us Duplicates in almost every Particular; so that in case one becomes useless, or lost, yet the other in great Measure supplies the Defect. Thus we have two Eyes, two Lobes of the Lungs, two Kidneys, two Testicles; so that one part remaining Vision, Respiration, Secretion, and Generation, are all performed. The Mahometan women, in the greatest part of Asia, destroy one Testicle. No doubt they find their Account in it; because the Males make their Addresses more frequently when there is a less Expence of Spirits at each Evacuation.

There is very little else in the book which at all brings Dover to life. An irrelevant remark, after he has told how he cured a man of smallpox who had almost died of it—"He is now living in South Wales, a Gentleman of £1000 per Annum"—may show his interest in money, or may merely be a further example of an old man's inability to keep to the point: and when he says " . . . though I cannot paint, yet I pretend to know a good picture", he is making a remark which many men have made.

But, in a final magnanimous gesture, he adds a note at the end of his book:

N.B. Having taken Notice of some Errors in the Practice of other Physicians, I shall frankly acknowledge one in my own: I have hitherto been too zealous in recommending one particular Apothecary; but am resolved, for the future, to let all my Patients make use of any Apothecary they like best; which, I think, is but doing Justice to the gentlemen of that Profession.

One wonders what effect this had upon the "particular Apothecary".

SIXTEEN

THUS, in one way and another, Thomas Dover irritated the medical profession of his day and gave them a variety of pretexts for returning his attacks. Yet the real gravamen of the charge against him, the target of an assault that was all but united, we have not yet reached. This is his panacea, the grounds for his nickname. All his other quirks, even his criticisms of his fellow medicos, were side-issues compared to his advocacy of mercury for the treatment of about half the diseases that came before him, and his reiterated statement that it did no harm. This claim provoked the learned as well as the prejudiced and the incompetent, and banded them against him.

There was nothing new about mercury as an item in the pharmacopoeia. Its use as an ingredient in pills and other medicines, and even in its crude form, was widespread in Dover's day: but there was intense disagreement as to its effects, both on the disease it was supposed to be curing and on the patient's general health.

Dover had no misgiving of any kind. He prescribed it freely in cases of consumption and apoplexy, in "hypochondriacal diseases", in green-sickness, and—a wide category—diseases of the stomach. He particularizes abundantly on its uses.

I have of late experienced that quick-silver is the most beneficial thing in all the world for the lungs, taking one ounce every morning.

It is valuable to the family:

The Indians at the Malucco Islands and the ladies at Smyrna often take quick-silver, as a remedy against barrenness. An ounce may be taken once a day for a month or two.

For apoplexy:

Take of Mercurius dulcis, cinnabar of antimony, each one scruple. Make into a bolus with conserve of hips.

It is in writing about the Green-sickness, however, that he gives his most deliberate defence of its virtues:

'Tis a generally received notion, nay, even amongst many gentlemen of the faculty, that quicksilver is poison. If such persons are not ashamed of being no better natural philosophers, I have no reason for being under confusion of face for them.

Their opinion is a sign they have travelled far at home.

Let them take a trip to Hungary, and visit the mines where the Quicksilver is dug; they may there see slaves working entirely naked to prevent the stealing this precious jelly of metals, as it may be called; yet every day swallow so much that they buy a choppin of drink with it at night.

Several Physicians have enquired of my patients, to what end do I give it? Wherein can the efficacy or power of it consist? If they do not know, what follows may serve for instruction.

First, it secures the patient from all vermicular diseases; of which no Physician can be sufficiently apprised, that has not spent some time in hot climates.

Next, it opens all obstructions, which are supposed to be another cause of diseases.

Lastly, it makes a pure balsam of the blood, beyond all other things in creation. Otherwise, why cannot venereal ulcers be cured without it? We often see those sores in a salivation grow well, without the help of a surgeon.

I desire to know why I am called "The Quicksilver Doctor" by way of derision? Pray do not you, Gentlemen Physicians, prescribe it almost every day of your lives? I aver you do. Only you disguise it; and I give it in such an open honest manner, that my patient cannot be deceived in taking it. Let me ask you, What is your Aethiop's Mineral? Is it not Quicksilver, ground to a black powder, with brimstone? And in as great esteem with you as any of your medicines? A very ingenious Physician says, "This is like striking a man with your sword in the scabbard"; and were it not possible to have found a worse menstrum than sulphur, I do not know whether it ought not even then to have been tried. Certainly this medicine shows a more than common virtue, which can thus powerfully exert itself, when bound down by so contrary a quality.

Much may be said to show the impossibility of Quicksilver doing any damage to the patient. What gives offence to Nature is what we term Spiculae, points or edges. Now, Quicksilver, always retaining a globular figure, together with the softness of its body, no harm can happen from the use of it . . .

Now does anything so useful, so beneficial to Mankind, deserve to be so much exploded, and treated with so much calumny? But among all their false insinuations, let them bring one single instance, well attested, of the damage anyone has received from it. Though I believe there never was a

medicine given, but has sometimes proved not only detrimental to the
patient, but even death itself has ensued, especially when misapplied . . .
I aver Quicksilver never did any harm to the patient, which is more than
can be said of any other medicine.

This is categorical enough; there is no need to quote further in
order to show the wholehearted enthusiasm he felt towards it. In
default of better knowledge, I think we may reasonably conclude that
it was the experiences of the privateering years which convinced Dover
of the virtues of mercury. The natural hazards of such a voyage, even
without the specific and—in his mind—clinching reference to venereal
disease, must almost certainly have given him the grounds for his
affection (there is a hint of this in the comments of Daniel Turner) ; and
the sardonic tinge to his thought, as indicated by the addition of
ipecacuanha to his famous Powder, could easily incline him to suspect
such disease as a probable contributor to almost all ill-health. At all
events, it would do no harm to act as if the enemy were present.

II

The first reply to *The Ancient Physician's Legacy* was written by a
surgeon named Bradley, who addressed his *Physical and Philosophical
Remarks* to the Company of Apothecaries in the same year. In the subtitle, Bradley explains that the book contains "Some animadversions
on his (Dover's) scurrilous treatment of the Professors of Physic in
general, with a word or two of the usefulness of his legacy to all private
families", and claims to show "That the Enthusiast and the Empirick
is not upon so good a foot as the scholar and the Physician; that the
former acts upon uncertainties, and the latter upon sure rules and
observations".

He goes on to accuse Dover of rancour and malice, of "invectives,
false insinuations and dogmatical decrees", and of an "ungentleman-
like way of treating mankind, together with his blind zealous boasting
of himself". In dealing with the cures which Dover advertised, Bradley
is either openly sceptical, or ridicules them because they are unexcep-
tional. He points to inconsistencies, "indecencies", and such similarities as occur between the stories told by Dover and those reputed to
have been told by other doctors. The book is entirely devoted to
destructive and detailed criticism, of which the following extracts are
typical:

I would gladly be informed what the poor patient is the better for knowing that the gout in his hand is called Chiragra, or in the foot Podagra, etc. . . . I will appeal to any understanding man whether his *ipse dixit* be a sufficient standard to induce mankind to believe the gout always begins in the first joint of the great toe, and that about mid-night.

If the world had made no more progress in the healing art than he has done, we must have been, of all wretches the most miserable, notwithstanding his forty-nine years' practice.

After speaking of Dover's treatment of the Itch, Bradley remarks:

But I fear our worthy author before us has an itch, which all the cold baths in Europe cannot heal, I mean that itch of the tongue which not being well cured in his youth became so inveterate as not to be rooted out.

The vaunted cures are pooh-poohed: "No-one in his senses can reasonably believe such a story. But this is a piece with all the rest."

He intersperses a quotation describing Dover's experiences at Guaiaquil with "Pray observe our Captain Bluster", and "A modest Captain indeed". Dover's integrity is attacked.

If he can but fill his own pockets he cares not by what means so ever he keeps others empty, tho' it be by wounding 'em in the most dangerous manner, even in their characters and reputation.

Coming to the entries on Green-sickness, the critic really enjoys himself.

Our learned author has made such a hotch-potch of this distemper as I never met with before; first laying the fault on the poor mothers for lacing their children too strait, which makes them crooked; then it gives them an appetite to old trunks, woollen rags, nut-shells, etc. Then he makes a digression and falls foul of the poor mothers again for not permitting their children to eat green fruit, which, he says, is the most wholesome and a great destroyer of worms. Then runs from his subject and falls foul of the faculty by asserting a notorious falsity, as he makes appear from his own words anon, and throws out his invectives against them in the usual manner . . . Then he tells you another idle story, which has all the appearances of a fable; of such a one told such a one, till he has totally lost the subject he first began; and concludes this chapter with two quotations . . . to confirm what all practitioners allow to be one of the best medicines in the whole materia medica. But I have hinted at this in the preceding chapter and am at a loss to know how private families will be benefited by this jargon.

*W*Hereas it hath of late been the Endeavour of several Members of the Physicians Colledg, to reform the [ab]uses of the Apothecaries, as well in the [pri]zes as in the Composition of their Medecines, [th]is is to give notice for the Publick Good, that [S]uperfine Sort of *Jesuits Bark* ready powder'd [and] paper'd into Doses with or without Di[re]ctions for the Use of it, is to be had at [Mr]. *Charles Goodal*'s, at the *Coach* and *Horses* in [Ph]yficians *Colledg* in *Warwick-Lane*, at 4 s. per [ou]nce, or for a Quantity together at 3 l. per [po]und; for the Reasonableness of which Prizes, [co]nfidering the Loss and Trouble in Powder[in]g) we appeal to all the *Druggists* and *Apotheca*[rie]s themselves in Town, and particularly to [M]r. *Thair*, Druggist in *Newgate-street*, to whom [w]e paid full 9 s. per Pound for a considerable [qu]antity for the Use of our self and our Friends. And for the *Excellency* and *Efficacy* of this par[ti]cular *Bark*, enquire of Dr. *Morton* in *Grey-Fryars*. I am to be spoken with (Prayers at S. Sepulchres) [ev]ery day, but the Lord's Day, at Seven in the Morning, [an]d at Home from Eight in the Morning till Ten at [N]ight.

[T]he *Poor* may have Advice (that is, Nothing) for Nothing.

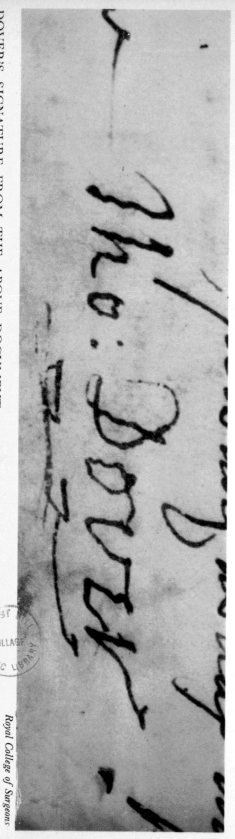

Bradley's one favourable comment is on Dover's free treatment of the workhouse children in Bristol: "The first laudable action I have yet met with from this practitioner."

III

A second book, likewise published in 1733, was an anonymous *Treatise on Mercury* "shewing the danger of taking it crude for all manner of disorders . . . with some remarks on the Ancient Physician's Legacy". The writer of this took a more temperate line.

Mercury may be ranked among the slow poisons if applied by the unskilful hand . . . My design is not to derogate from the virtues of Mercury, but to warn the reader against its misuse . . . The old maxim that what can do good may also do much harm, seems to be quite forgot, else people would not take Mercury, one of the most powerful medicines in nature almost for any complaints without considering age, sex, constitution, present situation of the body or all other circumstances; it is sufficient inducement for many to follow this practice, because it is such an easy remedy, and some have found benefit from it, or that it is now become fashionable. Thus Mercury reigns triumphant under the character of a panacea or universal medicine; and the public seems to be so zealous in recommending this Darling that I expect it may soon be preferred by the fair sex to their closets as a cordial.

He then gives an account of the history of the use of Mercury, and points out the disastrous effects it can have later in life. His references to the *Legacy* show that he considered that its danger lay in recommending mercury so generally to the public, who were entirely unaware of its dangers:

I dare to affirm this, that some nurses, and even the grave-diggers are obliged to him for it.

This author is unconvinced by Dover's accounts of its healing power in cases of the stone and diseases of the lung, and says that the assertion that it never did any harm is contradicted by his own reason and experience.

IV

In the fourth edition of the *Legacy*, which also appeared in 1733—a full year in the annals of medical controversy—Dover answers some of the criticisms brought against him. He challenges Bradley to show when he has lost three patients in the last five years in acute or chronic cases, gives a list of patients who will vouch for the effectiveness of his treatment, and adds several letters from patients who have been cured by him. The following is from Joseph Potts:

Though a stranger to the nature of quicksilver . . . I think I should be ungrateful to God and unjust to you and Mankind should I be silent amid the clamours and artifices which are made use of to lessen your reputation and deter the world from being benefited by one of the best of remedies, perhaps in Physick.

One letter, written in tones of heavy satire, deplores the devotion which has led Dover to publish facts which are so honest, and with so little consideration for his own welfare. It then comments on the characters of Dover's critics, and ridicules their ignorance. Dover concludes with a robust postscript to these testimonies.

I have taken it myself above six and forty years; I have been in all sorts of climates and am now upwards of seventy, and yet, I thank God, enjoy a perfect state of health . . . Give me leave to tell you Sir, that the world will think much better of me for owning my ignorance, than if I had led them as you have done, into a blind labyrinth of hard words and unintelligible terms.

V

The anonymous author of the *Treatise on Mercury* replied, and the interchange becomes increasingly petty. For instance:

I find that calling a story silly is your way of answering it,

and

But for the sake of the proverb *errare humanum* etc., which you know fits some better than others in this blundering age, I will not dwell any longer on this point.

Again,

You say if I had not mentioned the King, (in his description of a case) I should at least have said who was then Lord Mayor. I don't apprehend any joke in this, unless you took the Lord Mayor for the greater person of the two, or at least the King's equal.

And

Drawing now towards a conclusion you tell us, you cannot recommend so general and universal a use of it. How universal a use? That which you had recommended before, or that which I condemn? None, you continue, should venture on the use of Mercury, without the advice of some able person, who understands the nature of it. To this I readily agree, it being the chief drift of my treatise.

So the controversy continued, with such a passion and confusion of quotation and refutation that it is often difficult to know which side a particular paragraph is defending.

VI

The next publication was of much more weight, being almost three hundred pages of serious examination, by one Daniel Turner, of Dover's accounts of the various symptoms and treatments of diseases. Though a great proportion of this book is entirely medical in character, the personal attack is continued:

The gentleman, you will find by all his prescriptions, is for striking at the root, and rather than not destroy the disease, he will kill the patient . . .

I will now come to his cure, such as most surely none, unless a farrier, would have prescribed; his conversation, you know, has been much with tars, and he thinks that the most tender constitutions of our citizens will bear the same rough handling.

Turner's main objections are that the cures are either too obvious to be worth writing about, or too absurd to be credible. In the case of King's Evil, however, he gives Dover credit:

His method of cure is one of the best he has laid down, and as likely to do some good as many others we have had communicated for so stubborn a malady.

This, it is interesting to note, was one of the diseases for which Dover had prescribed Mercury.

After his detailed examination, Turner concludes:

In justice to the Public I must declare, that as the practical part thereof is most absurd, so the historical part the most romantic I have ever met withal; it may serve to amuse the ignorant, for whom doubtless it was intended, but can never pass with men of any tolerable understanding. You see plainly that it will not go down with that of Daniel Turner.

Daniel Turner's "Impartial Survey" of *The Ancient Physician's Legacy* was sufficiently strong to drive Dover underground. The next move in the game was a book entirely devoted to the subject of Quicksilver. It was called "*The Encomium Argenti Vivi*: a treatise upon the use and properties of quick-silver, with some remarks upon the animadversions of Dr. Turner upon Belloste". Ostensibly the work of "a gentleman of Trinity College, Cambridge", it is obviously written by Dover himself. He remarks on the recent extraordinary increase in the use of Mercury and says that now, " 'tis as usual to meet with in families as snuff or tobacco", but denies that he ever regarded it as the cure for all diseases:

A universal medicine is nonsense; no one can be alike good in all cases ... I need not therefore say I question whether there is such another medicine in the world: no-one will affirm there is.

He then gives an account of the nature and properties of Mercury, its natural history and chemical uses, and the varieties of forms in which it is used by doctors:

The greatest objection that I know against it is, that several dabblers in Physic have done harm with it; but with what medicine have they not? ... Every medicine in such hands is like a sword in a mad-man's, but with the skilful and understanding who know how to make a proper use of it, it has been found to do surprising things.

He regards himself as a pioneer, whose work is met with the scorn always directed at innovations.

It is a difficult matter to remove vulgar errors; they are as strongly rooted as the most inveterate disease, and reason and physic are frequently baffled by both. How high did the cry run formerly against the use of Bark, one of the best medicines in the materia medica! What fears! What apprehensions! of its evil consequences! What strange misconstructions of its effects!

Then comes a familiar line of argument:

All great Doctors from Hippocrates, Aesculapius to Freind (a well-known seventeenth-century doctor) have met opposition at first. It only remains for such to proceed upon their own strength; a genius will see further into nature in the compass of a few years than ordinary souls were they to live a thousand.

The inference is obvious: we need not look far for the genius. The next step is to regard most of the opposition as personal rather than scientific: "As some are made enemies by envy, others may become so through interest." If a new medicine became widely used, "How many phials might be thrown to the dung-hills." Many of his opponents add hypocrisy to habitude and obscurantism. They pretend to be violently against the use of mercury, while secretly using it in their own preparations.

But those who set out upon different principles, who consider Physic, not as a Trade, but as a Science, a useful and an honourable one, and intend the good of mankind by Profession never act thus in the dark; their practice is very fair and open, and friends they are to those, who like themselves are content with the reputation of doing good, and borrow not assistances from Cabal and Parties to steal a name. Such was Dr. Freind, and such are several now living, ornaments of the Faculty, and most useful members of Society.

Wholly unconscious of irony, he follows up these charges of disingenuousness by speaking of himself in the third person, and linking his name with that of Belloste, a former advocate of the use of mercury.

Thomas Dover and Mr. Belloste have acted very fairly and very honestly in laying the advantages of Mercury before Mankind . . . Experience is the best guide, and facts the strongest recommendation; these gentlemen have found it useful and accordingly openly declare what relief they have found it to give. It is an easy matter to cry out Quack! Empirick! but the world will still think such men as honest, as skilful, who prove their practice by well attested facts. This is the case with these two gentlemen; Cabals and Factions are known to subsist among the Faculty; and it may be much safer to kill in the common road of practice, than cure out of it. Clamours are very apt to rise and falsehoods to fly about when Physicians shall dare to be greater friends to the patient than the Apothecary.

This book was followed by two more of little interest, one being a review of the whole controversy, by a Mercurialist, and another in defence of Dr. Turner by a Country Physician. Dover's book was translated into French in 1734, and his arguments became well known on the Continent. In 1762 Professor Trenchin edited the *Opera Omnia* of Bellonius of Geneva, and in a laudatory dedication to Dover praised him as one of the most distinguished Physicians of the time.

And there, perhaps, we may leave the argument.

VII

There, too, whether we like it or not, we must leave Thomas Dover. This was his final blaze of fame, his last fandango. After the early seventeen-thirties, he fades from public view. We know that for a while he continued to practise, moving first to Lombard Street, and then to Arundel Street off the Strand; but he was an old man now, he did less and less work, and spent more of his time at his friend Tracy's house in Gloucestershire. There, in 1742, he died, and was buried in the churchyard of Stanway.

Dr. Nixon, whom we have quoted on Dover's earlier life, supplies the final evidence in the *Proceedings of the Royal Society of Medicine*, Vol. 6, 1913:

. . . The tombstone popularly supposed in Barton to be that of Thomas Dover turns out, on close inspection (it is nearly indecipherable), to be erected in memory of "William Sands, who sailed round the world with Dr. Dover". This stone stands against the outside of the chancel wall at Barton on the north side. There is an entry in the register of Stanway, in Gloucestershire, stating that Thomas Dover, M.B., was buried there on April 20, 1742.

I have found two contemporary references to his death:—(1) *The Oracle or Bristol Weekly Messenger*, i. Saturday, May 1, 1742, No. 5, under domestic occurrences: London, April 27, from the general Evening Post: Deaths—Dr. Thomas Dover, in Warwickshire.

(2) *London Magazine*, April, 1742, p. 206: "Dr. Thomas Dover, famous

for administering quicksilver to his patients, in the 85th year of his age."
The last years of Dr. Dover's life were spent at Stanway House (now the
seat of Lord Elcho), with his friend Robert Tracy, to whom he dedicated
his famous book "The Ancient Physician's Legacy to his Countrymen".
He was buried at his own request in the vault belonging to the Tracy
family. This vault is situated under the altar but no memorials remain of
the family or of Dover in the church . . .

A life of eighty years, eventful, colourful, strenuous with conflict
and adventure; it is tantalizing to see how little they have left us of the
man who lived them. Only the faintest thread remains to link together
the few vivid years that glitter across two centuries. True, we might be
worse off. Many men who shone in Dover's day have left us nothing.
Yet it is peculiarly vexing to have so little and yet so much; so many
actions with so little motive to explain them; so many facts, with so
little to give them meaning. Truth, it has been said, lies not in the facts
but in the pattern which we make from them, the pattern which gives
them coherence. In this sense of the word we do not know the truth
about Dover. We do not know what sort of man he was. We know only
certain things that he did. Even his signature on a document dated
6 May, 1727, adds hardly anything to our knowledge. The script of an
elderly man of the period, it shows certain traces of a rather crabbed
individuality of which we had plenty of evidence already.

The evidence all seems to point one way. An egotist, strong willed
and intelligent, Dover had the good luck to fall in with a great man and
be influenced by him. Like many of his kind, he was receptive so long as
new experience impressed him. After his return from the famous voyage
we can deduce no more than that his practical work grew more assured
and skilful: and this only because he asks his critics to look at the last
ten years—i.e. 1723 onwards.

He was contentious, and quick-tempered, but the few writers who
have studied his life seem to have too readily accepted the reports of his
ill temper and the impossibility of getting on with him. Even according
to the testimony of Woodes Rogers, who had no cause to love him, it
is clear that he had many supporters in the ships' company. On one
occasion at least, Cooke sided with him. He could behave with decision and courage, and, it appears, he could avoid action in a manner
that must seem unadventurous as long as we do not know his reasons.
He could take charge in a crisis, and for his success in dealing with the
terrifying incidence of plague among the crews we are not obliged to
rely on his own account.

This is perhaps as well. Where he refers more than once to his medical successes, the tale does not lose in the repetition; Drs. Ernest Hart and Dawson Williams point this out in their note (*B.M.J.* Vol. I, 1897) on the various editions of *The Ancient Physician's Legacy*.

It is interesting to compare the testimonials to Dover by grateful patients as they are printed in the different editions of his book. As time went on the author improved these, if he left untouched the other parts of his work. There is a testimonial from one Will. Moses of Lewisham: in the later editions a postscript is added which does not appear in the earlier ones. "P.S.—I have removed from Greenwich to Lewisham: shall always be proud to kiss your Hand." Another patient, in the early editions, says, "I think it my duty to return you my hearty Thanks"; later on this has grown into "ten million of thanks".

We remember, too, how Dover gave himself the sole credit for taking Guaiaquil.

Of his medical work the consensus of professional opinion since his time is that he was a pioneer who did far more good than harm. We do not know how many of his patients suffered from gingivitis and more serious complaints after being dosed with mercury, but we can see clearly enough that contemporary depreciation of his cures cannot be swallowed whole. Much of his treatment makes good sense today: most was ahead of all but the foremost work of his time: and his powder is still in use, after more than two hundred years.

The powder—recommended in *The Ancient Physician's Legacy* for the treatment of gout—has in recent times been given in doses of ten to fifteen grains. The dose Dover himself prescribed was forty to sixty or seventy grains. He was aware that this dose was large:

Some apothecaries have desired their patients to make their wills and settle their affairs before they venture on so large a dose as from 40 to 70 grains.

The powder was made in the following way:

Take Opium one Ounce, Salt-Petre and Tartar vitriolated, each four Ounces, Ipecacuana one Ounce. Put the Salt-Petre and Tartar into a red hot Mortar, stirring them with a spoon till they have done flaming—Then powder them very fine; after that, slice your Opium; grind these to a Powder, and then mix the other Powders with these. Dose from 40 to 60 or 70 grains in a glass of white wine Posset (made by adding port or sherry

to milk and curdling it) going to bed, covering up warm and drinking a
quart or three pints of the Posset. Drink while sweating.

Dover was not a Sydenham or a Radcliffe, but he was on the right
lines in applying observation and logic to medicine, as they did. He was
generous of his time and labour, and at Bristol workhouses he treated
the poor for nothing.

Of his inner life we know only that he regarded God as the source
of all knowledge. Of his domestic life we know nothing. We dare not
assert that he saw to the reprint of the *Annalia*, and so cannot claim
for him scholarship and familial piety. Still, he may have done it. We
know nothing of him as husband and father. He was cantankerous in
argument, but bore himself no worse than his opponents. He could
make friends. One, Sydenham, shared a house with him when he was
young; another, Tracy, when he was old. Many able and honest men
have worse records.

M

ANNALIA DUBRENSIA

For the benefit of the curious, the following details are drawn from a study of three copies of this book—two of 1636, and one the 1700 reprint. A fourth copy, also dated 1636, is no longer available in the Museum. There is no trace at all of the extra poem in either of the two earlier editions.

1. *The first 1636 edition.*

This is bound together with a poem, *Cooper's Hill*, by John Denham, Esq., dated 1655. On the leather cover is a crest, with the name Rt. Honble Thos Grenville. A hand-written note is slipped into the book, on a separate piece of paper (obviously written some considerable time ago)—"Dover Annalia Dubrensia/4° 1636/ This book now grown very scarce is rarely to be found with the original frontispiece as in this copy. I have not seen any other which like this has a printed presentation title, with the autograph of the Editor."

The first printed page has on it "For the much Honoured/ Sr. Thomas Trevor Knight,/ one of the Barons of/ the Exchequer." Hand-written at the top of the page is "1640", and at the bottom "Robt. Dover his/ Presentation", in small, neat writing, with flourishes of the capitals.

This is rather a narrow copy, so that the frontispiece is folded over and the print runs right up to the left-hand edge of each page. The frontispiece is opposite the title page. It shows a stretch of country, with Robert Dover on horseback in the foreground, the castle in the background (or, more accurately, at the top of the picture, since each item is separate, and scarcely seems related to the next), and groups of people engaged in various activities—a man standing on his head, others feasting round a table, men on horseback hunting, dogs chasing a hare, etc. On the next page, after the title page, is Walbancke's dedicatory letter.

2. *Another 1636 edition.*

The binding of this copy is obviously of later date. It is bound together with *The History of the Ancient and moderne Estate of the Principality of Wales, Dutchy of Cornewall, and Earldome of Chester. 1630.* The pages are not so closely trimmed, and the frontispiece is unfolded. Nothing is printed before the frontispiece and the title page.

3. *The 1700* (?) *reprint.*

This copy is bound in leather, with the crest *Honi soit qui mal y pense* and GIIIR on the cover. It appears to have been printed from the same blocks as the other two copies, though the print is sharper and less liable to blur. There is no fly leaf. The book opens straight on the title page. This is followed by the dedicatory letter, after which comes the reference to Dr. Dover's duty to his grandfather. A complete blank sheet is then followed by the frontispiece, after which the order is the same as in the other two copies.

A closer inspection revealed several textual variations:

1 & 3 have a poem "To my noble *Friend* Mr. Robert Dover".

No. 2 has "noble Freind"—a printer's error, since the word is spelt correctly in other places.

1 & 2 have on p. 6 of the text, at the bottom, "First" as the first word to follow on the next page. 3 corrects this, and puts "He" (spelt "hee" in the poem).

1 & 2, at the bottom of the page marked D, give the first word on the following page as "Happy". 3 gives "The" (Thenot, the character whose speech starts at the top of the next page).

1 & 2, in an anagram poem on the page before F, have at the foot of the poem "Robertus Doverus/ Anagramma:/ Do Robur et Versus". 3 has "Rob*ret*us Doverus,/ Anagramma:/ Doroburetve*b*sus", making nonsense of the anagram.

1 & 2, in another anagram on p.   H.3, have

Verus Rubor Dotes ⎱	Ana
Robertus Doverus ⎰	

3 has

Verus *Rober* Dotes ⎱	Ana.
Robertus Doverus ⎰	

The third poem from the end is signed R. Newburgh in No. 1, and simply R.N. in 2 & 3.

In No. 3 the word Finis is placed after the extra poem, instead of after the Heywood poem which ends the other two volumes.

Extracts from the extra poem in the 1700 reprint of the Annalia Dubrensia

In Celebration of the yearely Preserver of the Games at Cotswald

Heare me you men of strife! you that have bin,
Long time maintain'd by the dull Peoples sin,
At Lyon's, Furnifold's and Clement's Inne!

With huge, o're-comming Mutton, Target-Cheese,
Beefe, that the queasie stomack'd Guard would please,
And limber Groats, full halfe a Score for Fees. . . .

. . . Ere you a Yeare are dead, your Sonnes shall watch,
And rore all Night with Ale, in house of Thatch;
And spend, 'till Swords are worne in Belts of Match.

Whilst Dover[1] (that his knowledge not Imploy's
T'increase his Neighbours Quarrels, but their Joyes;)
Shall in his age, get Money, Girles, and Boyes! . . .

. . . His Girles, shall dow'r-lesse wed with Heires of birth;
His Boyes, plough London Widowes up like earth:
Whilst Cotswald Bards caroll their Nuptiall Mirth!

Dover (the Gentry's Darling) know this flame,
Is but a willing tribute to the Game,
Sung by a Poet that conceals his name.

This poem the D.N.B. attributes to D'Avenant. It does not say on what grounds, and I have been unable to find them.

---

[1] He was bred an Attorney, who never try'd but two Causes, always made up the Difference.

173

Cooke gives the following details of the cargo of the Acapulco ship. (Original spelling.)

Allejars	82 pieces	Petticoats	265 pieces
Atlasses	52 ,,	Quilts	14 ,,
Basts	188 ,,	Romols	548 ,,
Cottoneas	291 ,,	Ribbons divers sorts	6834 ,,
Calicoes white	6603 ,,	Ribbons flowered with	
Calicoes coloured	4372 ,,	gold and silver	481 ,,
Counterpoints		Silk stockings	4310 ,,
divers sorts	206 ,,	Silk raw of China	28502 ,,
Coffaes	270 ,,	thrown	11990 ,,
Chints	24289 ,,	sewing	1370 ,,
Chint Sashes	24 ,,	Bengal	61 ,,
Chelloes	362 ,,	sleeve	6581 ,,
Charadorees	18 ,,	fringes	194 ,,
China flowered silks	5 ,,	Soofeys	115 ,,
Damasks	120 ,,	Stockings cotton	1084 ,,
Dimities	460 ,,	Sannoes	425 ,,
Diapers	77 ,,	Satins and Taffaties	
Elatches	3106 ,,	divers sorts	7008 ,,
Fans	5806 ,,	Satins and Taffaties with	
Gurrahs	1180 ,,	gold and silver	192 ,,
Ginghams	263 ,,	Silk divers sorts	511 ,,
Guinea Stuffs	235 ,,	Silk sashes	341 ,,
Hum hums	105 ,,	Sashes calico	544 ,,
Handkerchiefs pieces	38 ,,	Silk gowns	37 ,,
,, single	157 ,,	Tanbes	454 ,,
Long cloth	2577 ,,	Musk	5997 ,,
Mulmuls	55 ,,	Cinnamon	9710 ,,
Neckcloths	123 ,,	Cloves	1182 ,,
Nillaes	580 ,,	Benjamen	3300 ,,
Niccaneas	8020 ,,	Beeswax	152 ,,
Photees	152 ,,	Gum elemia	120 ,,
Pelongs	1236 ,,	China ware, several chests & jars	
Paunches	16561 ,,	Several parcels of odd things	
Palampores	4053 ,,		

APPENDIX D

The following is Woodes Rogers's detailed account of the plague:

May 11. A fresh gale at S.S.W. We had upwards of 20 Men that fell ill within these 24 Hours, our Consort near 50, of a malignant Fever, contracted as I suppose at *Guiaquil*, where I was informed, that about a Month or 5 weeks before we took it, a contagious Disease which raged there swept off 10 or 12 Persons every Day for a considerable Time; so that the Floors of all the Churches (which are their usual Burial Places) were fill'd so fast, that they were obliged to dig a large and deep Hole of about a Rod Square, close by the great Church, where I kept guard; and this Hole was almost fill'd with Corps half putrified. The Mortality was so very great, and our lying so long in the Church surrounded with such unwholesome Scents, was enough to infect us too.

Capt. *Courtney* was taken ill, and Capt. *Dover* went on board the *Duchess* to prescribe for him.

May 15. At 6 last Night Mr. *Samuel Hopkins*, Dr. *Dover's* Kinsman and Assistant, died . . .

May 17 . . . Our Men in both Ships continue very ill; we have near 60 sick, and the *Duchess* upwards of 80.

May 18 . . . *Edward Downe* died at 12 at Night.

May 19 . . . About 10 in the Morning *James Daniel* our Joiner died . . .

May 21 . . . This Day *Tho. Hughes* a very good Sailor died, as did Mr. *George Underhill* . . . About the same Time another young Man, call'd *John English*, died aboard the *Haver de Grace*, and we have many still sick. If we had staid in the Harbour, we should in all probability have lost near half of our Men.

May 22 . . . At 9 last Night *Jacob Scronder* a *Dutch*-man, and very good Sailor, died . . .

May 23 . . . Last Night died *Law. Carney* of a malignant Fever. There is hardly a Man in the Ship, who had been ashore at *Guayaquil* but has felt something of this Distemper, whereas not one of those that were not there have been sick yet. Finding that Punch did preserve my own Health, I prescribed it freely among such of the Ship's Company as were well, to preserve theirs.

May 25 . . . Last Night *Peter Marshal* a good sailor died . . .

. . . *Thomas Morgan*, a *Welch* Land-man, died the 31st of May; *George Bishop*, another Land-man, the 4th of June . . .

Cooke records the plague and its source, but has little else to say.

175

Annalia Dubrensia: ed. 1636 by Matthew Walbancke.
Another copy, imperfect, without frontispiece: now missing.
Another edition. R. Raworth for M. Walbancke, 1636: reprinted by Robert Dover's grandson, 1700.
Another edition, ed. by A. B. Grosart in 1877, with notes. Privately printed in Manchester, 52 copies only.
Reprinted and edited with notes by E. R. Vyvyan in 1878 at Cheltenham.
* ANONYMOUS: *A Country Physician's Reply to the Quick-Silver Controversy.*
* ANONYMOUS: *A Treatise on Mercury.*
ANONYMOUS MEDICAL TRACTS. *An Essay on Physic.* 1673.
The Apothecaries' Vindication. 1676.
The Modern Quack. 1724.
The Modern Family Physician. 1776. Dublin.
BESANT, SIR WALTER: *London in the Eighteenth Century.* 1902.
BRADLEY, H.: *Remarks on Dr. Dover's "A.P.L.".* 1733.
BRISTOL: An account of the Hospitals, Almshouses and Public Schools in Bristol, 1775.
BRISTOL RECORD SOCIETY: *Bristol Corporation of the Poor,* Vol. 1. 1932.
CHAMBERLAYNE, EDWARD: *Angliae Notitia, or The Present State of England.* London. 1669–1724.
COOKE, EDWARD: *A Voyage to the South Sea.* 1712.
CORNMAN, FRANCIS: *Some Old London Shop Signs.* 1894. Privately printed.
Dictionary of National Biography.
DOVER, THOMAS: *The Ancient Physician's Legacy.* 1733. London.
Encomium Argenti Vivi. No date.
Legs d'un Ancien medecin a sa patrie. A la haye, chez Henri Scheurleer. 1734.
"Further notes on Thomas Dover." (*Proc. Roy. Soc. Med.:* Hist. Sect., 1913, pp. 233–7.)
"Dover's Ancient Physician's Legacy." (*B.M.J.,* 1897, I, 671–2.)
DOWNIE, WM.: "Chiefly concerning Dr. Dover of powder fame." (*Glasgow M.J.,* 1920, XCIII, 112–26.)
DUGDALE, SIR W.: *Antiquities of Warwickshire.* 1730.
ELOESSER, L.: "Pirate and Buccaneer Doctors." In *Annals of Medical History,* 1926, Vol. VIII, p. 45.
Encyclopaedia Britannica.
GARRISON, F. H., A.B., M.D.: *An Introduction to the History of Medicine.* 4th edition. 1929. Philadelphia and London.
GOSSE, SIR E.: *Seventeenth Century Studies.* 1897. Cambridge.

* These books are not dated, but were probably all printed in 1733 or 1734.

HARLEIAN SOCIETY PUBLICATIONS: Vol. 5. "Providence Displayed", by Alexander Selkirk. 1745. Vol. 62. "Visitation of Warwickshire", 1. 1682.

HOWELL, T. H.: "Dover's Legacy." *Edin. Med. J.*, 1942, Vol. XLIX, pp. 266-8.

HUTCHINSON, B.: *Biographica Medica*. London. 1799.

LATIMER, JOHN: *The Annals of Bristol in the 17th Century.*
The Annals of Bristol in the 18th Century.

MANDEVILLE, BERNARD DE, D.D.: *A Treatise on Hypochondriac and Hysteric Passions*. London. 1730.

Mercurialist: A Short Review of the Quick-Silver Controversy.

MONRO, T. K.: *The Physician as man of letters, science and action*. 2nd edition. 1951.

MUNK, WM.: *Roll of the Royal College of Physicians.*

NEWMAN, SIR GEORGE, K.C.B., M.D., D.C.L.: *Thomas Sydenham : Reformer of English Medicine*. British Periodicals Ltd., 1924.

NIXON, J. A., M.B., M.R.C.P.: "Thomas Dover. Physician and Adventurer". Reprinted from the *Bristol Medico-Chirurgical Journal*, March 1909.
"Thomas Dover. Physician and Navigator." Reprinted from the *Bristol Medico-Chirurgical Journal*, March 1913.
"Salt Water Surgeons." *Lancet*, 1941, Vol. II, p. 774.

OSLER, SIR WILLIAM, M.B., M.R.C.P.: *An Alabama Student*. Oxford. 1908.

PAYNE, J. F., M.D. Oxon.: *Masters of Medicine : Thomas Sydenham*. T. Fisher Unwin, 1900.

PHEAR, D. N., M.D., B.Chir. *Thomas Dover, M.D.: Journal of the History of Medicine and Allied Sciences*. Yale, April 1954.

QUACK MEDICINES: A Collection of One Hundred and Eighty-Five Advertisements, chiefly relating to Quack Medicines. 1660.

RIDDELL, W. R.: "The Ancient Physician, and his legacy to his country." *Canada Lancet Pract.*, 1930, 74, 57-66.

RIESMAN, DAVID, M.D.: *Thomas Sydenham*. Paul B. Hoeber, Inc. N.Y. 1926.

RUDDER: *History of Gloucester*. 1779. London.

RUSSELL: "Thomas Dover, 1660-1742." *Edin. Med. J.*, 1942, Vol. XLIX, pp. 259-65.

STEELE, SIR RICHARD: *The Englishman*. No. 26. Dec. 3rd, 1714.

STOW, JOHN: *A Survey of London*. 6th edition, ed. and enlarged by J. Strype. London. 1755.

TURNER, DANIEL: The "A.P.L." Impartially Surveyed.

VENN, JOHN: *Biographical History of Gonville and Caius*. Cambridge. 1877.

WOOD, ANTONY À: *Athenae Oxoniensis*. Ed. Bliss.

ROGERS, WOODES: *A Cruising Voyage Around the World*. London. 1712.
2nd Edition with new material, 1718.
A Cruising Voyage Round the World. Edited with an Introduction by G. E. Manwaring, 1928.

INDEX

Q4